Exposing the Seduction of Disloyalty

Jerry A. Grillo, Jr

FZM Publishing
Copyright 2009
"Exposing the Seduction of Disloyalty"
By Fogzone Ministries
P.O. Box 3707 Hickory, NC. 28603

All rights reserved under International Copyright Law. Contents and/or cover may not be reproduced in whole or in part in any form without the express written consent of the publisher.

All Scriptures, unless indicated, are taken from the King James Version.

Scripture quotations marked NJKV are taken from the New King James Version.

Scripture quotations marked NIV are taken from the New International Version.

ISBN
978-0-9977689-5-4

Printed in the United States of America.

Special Thanks

First, I give thanks to my wonderful family. Maryann, you are truly the best wife I could have; your wisdom and counsel are golden. To my children, Jerry III and Jordan, there are no human words to describe how much I love you. I can whole heartedly say these three make my life worth living.

April Mercer, your dedication to the completion of this book is truly appreciated. Because of your hard work, I believe people will be blessed by, "Exposing the Seduction of Disloyalty." Your input has been an incredible help.

I want to thank every proofreader for their love and support. One day, I hope to read the books you will write.

The graphic work, and friendship, of Kingdom Vizion has helped to make this project a joy.

To my partners, thank you for sowing financially into Fogzone ministries. I also give a very special thank you to the members of The Favor Life Church; your love and confidence in allowing me to write this book is greatly appreciated.

To my parents, you are the greatest! and, I love spending time with you! Your prayers are very important as well as coveted. Finally, to my second set of parents, though some would call you "in-laws," I call you family.

Table of Contents

ENDORSEMENTS 9

INTRODUCTION 13

PREFACE 17

WHO IS JEZEBEL? 23

FIVE MOST DAMAGING INSURRECTIONISTS 41

CONFRONTING THE SPIRIT OF DISLOYALTY 75

THE PORTRAIT OF THE SPIRIT OF CONTROL 97

LOYALTY IS A RARE GIFT 115

EIGHT STAGES OF DISLOYALTY 127

SIGNS OF DISLOYALTY 145

WHY YOU NEED A PASTOR 159

CLOSING THOUGHTS 173

ENDORSEMENTS

The spirit of Jezebel is cancerous, contagious, and deadly to the vision of every spiritual leader. This spirit is like a snake whose head is hidden and almost impossible to find. Every Leader must read this book. Believe it. Keep it on your desk for the next 90 days.
    Dr Mike Murdock
    The Wisdom Center
    Dallas, TX

The men at my church, along with the "Men of Honor," can agree that the lessons contained in, "Exposing the Seduction of Disloyalty," which Dr Grillo taught, was on point; it revolutionized my church. As the Lord used Dr Grillo to penetrate our hearts, I've never seen so many men, liked spanked babies, cry out.

Dr Grillo asked the question, **"Are you a predator or a partner?"** Silence permeated the entire sanctuary as each man searched his heart to see if he was one, or the other.

Dr Grillo enlightened and taught us about the **five different Insurrectionists**: Lucifer, Absalom, Jezebel, Ahab, and Judas. We were glued to his presentation as he explained the Stages of Disloyalty; Witchcraft and Rebellion; and, the Signs of Disloyalty.

Due to their dire need of thirst, as the alter call was made, I saw what seemed like a herd of cattle rushing to a water hole. Before the words came out of Dr Grillo's mouth, the altar was full, to capacity.

Like us, you are guaranteed to be blessed and moved to a new dimension. Don't just take my word for it—receive this insightful wisdom on "Exposing the Seduction of Disloyalty."
    Bishop Harvey Bee
    Christian Fellowship Church
    Warner Robins, GA

Bishop Grillo is fast becoming a leading voice of authority regarding the different spirits within the church.

Having him minister at our Emotional Healing Conference became a valuable training session to our leadership. It was a needed breakthrough to many of our members.

To say that Bishop Grillo is qualified to pen these pages would be an understatement. It would also be a mistake to leave this book unread. You hold in your hand a key to unlocking the life God desires for you. With the least bit of expectation, I dare you to turn the pages of this book. God will begin to show out in your life!
    Bishop Jeff Poole
    New Hope International
    Warner Robins, GA

The Spirit of Disloyalty is a silent force holding back the church from walking in the power and purpose of God. In this book, Dr Grillo masterfully exposes the influence of the Jezebel spirit. He equips the body of Christ to deal with her evil character so that it can be

cast out, **FOREVER**; all for the purpose of reigning in the Kingdom of God. I highly recommend this book.
>
> Pastor Tyronne Stowe
> Former NFL Linebacker
> Gospel 4 Life Church
> Phoenix AZ

EXPOSING THE SEDUCTION OF DISLOYALTY

Introduction

Wrong people can create wrong seasons in our lives.

To avoid frustration, and delayed harvests, we must be able to discern who we allow to hang around us, who we allow to work with us, as well as, who we allow to know our secrets. I've learned, I am not obligated to change a deceiver, however, I am obligated to discern one and move swiftly away from him.

"Discernment is when your spirit is telling you something your mind isn't."

The ability to discern people will better equip a person to protect themselves from an enemy whose desire is to tear down, destroy vision, weaken focus, and break one's spirit. And, incorrect discernment can create a season of depression, dissension, and discouragement. Wrong people are the enemy's number one focus breaker. The devil does not destroy ministries, People Do! A Pastor who gets caught up in an immoral situation can destroy his ministry. And, sheep who give ear to wrong voices, and who begin to think wrongly, tend to become disloyal. At this point, it is possible for the Church, along with its ministry, to be hurt.

One reason I believe relational splits, church splits, and ministry wars occur is due to people being allowed to continue in ministry when correction is needed; the issues were not addressed in a timely fashion to ensure the problem was resolved. Also, some people have wormed their way into ministry for the purpose of promoting an agenda other than the ministry of the Lord Jesus Christ. Unfortunately, these individuals like being in control. In this book, I will be introducing five insurrectionist personalities. I will also attempt to instruct leaders in how they can defeat this enemy so they are no longer part of their lives.

I have titled this book, "Exposing the Seduction of Disloyalty," because the insurrectionist spirit tends to be disloyal in ministry. It is important to recognize the traits of a disloyal leader as well as to learn how to overcome their divisive ways. I heard a quote that seems to fit this manuscript, "If we don't have loyalty, we are no better than the beast at the door." So, for the beast to avoid ministry's door, it is vital that loyalty be taught, and practiced, across the board.

An insurrectionist spirit is not positioning himself to stand behind the pulpit nor is he looking for a leadership role. His goal is to control both from behind the scenes. They have serpent like qualities which can go unnoticed for long periods of time. Unfortunately, when they are exposed, the venom of their bite has, in most cases, already done its damage. They must be brought into the open quickly, then placed under supervision, or they could be asked to leave. If repentance has been observed, it is possible for them to be restored to ministry.

One way to deal with a venomous snake is to cut off its head; not a pleasant undertaking, for sure. However, it is rare for a person who has been operating under a controlling spirit to be restored to a leadership role. It is even more rare for them to return to a place of submission under those who are in authority. It is not impossible to restore a religious, disloyal person, but rare. My desire, through this book, is to impart ways in which to deal with the insurrectionist spirit.

In my opinion, this type of spirit cannot change; it is evil. It has the power to beguile and to seduce people into hating those in whom they once agreed. It is imperative this spirit be dethroned immediately, otherwise, it will apprehend weak individuals along with those who are dissatisfied with the current leadership. Silencing its voice is the only option that will prevent the enemy from killing, stealing, or destroying a congregation. Do not be passive! and, do not align yourself with this demonic personality.

I have been carrying this book, within my heart, for quite some time; however, after watching ministry's deal with false prophets, as well as these disloyal spirits, I have been prompted to declare war. It is time to stand up and be informed! It is time to say, No More! We are not going to allow this spirit to control our congregations, we are not going to be ignorant of its devices any longer.

After twenty-five years of experience in ministry, I believe this book will help silence the voices bringing a spirit of disloyalty to the Church.

WHOEVER HAS YOUR EAR HAS YOUR FUTURE!

Dr Jerry A. Grillo, Jr

Preface

I have read many books regarding the spirits of Jezebel and insurrection; both personalities like sitting among church members. One book is entitled, "Confronting the Jezebel." In "Exposing the Seduction of Disloyalty," I will expose the spirits of Jezebel and disloyalty.

When someone becomes disloyal, they begin to operate out of a spirit of rebellion. When this happens, they can be mistrusting and critical of the **main Pastor** and all he is doing, as well as the direction he is taking the church.

It is my goal to reveal five different personalities that can operate in disloyal people. I will describe them and give solutions on how they must be dealt with.

I believe the Church has been wounded by disloyal people and would greatly benefit from spiritual healing. On multiple occasions, I've listened to the stories of wounded people within the House of God; horror stories of mistreatment and belittlement occurring in the name of religion. Many of these stories came from Pastors, Bishops, and Worship Leaders. Most described how the active members of the Church were abused by the "pew-sitter" who lacked the sense of responsibility, or initiative, to be helpful in their organization.

Never has there been such hatred. Never has there been such cold, calloused feelings as when a person turns away from their pastor. When this happens, disconnecting from the Pastor's teaching is immediate. They begin to question the Pastor's authority as well as his leadership; this is where the spirit of disloyalty begins to deceive.

Though there are probably more than five insurrectionists in the Bible, I believe the five listed, in this book, are the doors for all the others to walk through.

I have faced every one of these enemies; they drained and wearied me to the point of wanting to leave the ministry. As I pulled out the daggers of hate and anger that came from people I believed were "holy" and "called," I could only cry. Disloyal people don't leave in a quiet manner nor do they leave in an orderly fashion; however, when they do leave, they leave a trail of pain behind. These problems will not go away on their own and running from them is not an option either. The real solution comes through powerful partnership. Elijah understood the importance of having strong partners so, he anointed three men who were significant in the destruction of those opposed to the gospel.

Hear me! and, hear me clearly! Without the power of the Holy Spirit and the needed courage to boldly confront the insurrectionist, it is nearly impossible to win any fight against disloyalty. Running from the battle, bowing out of it, or trying to make peace will not do; implementing this defeatist strategy can devour your spirit, cause your business or church to be taken over, and it can destroy your ministry.

A spirit of disloyalty can exist in your immediate family; I know this to be true. When children are in the leadership role, it can be difficult for the parents to walk in submission to their child's authority. And, because of jealousy, siblings also struggle to submit to each other in these instances. It is important to guard against jealousy by not allowing wrong thoughts, or attitudes, to dictate whether you submit, or not.

Miriam's Disloyalty

The book of Exodus referred to Miriam as a prophetess and she was also the sister of Moses.
"Then Miriam the prophetess, the sister of Aaron, took the timbrel in her hand; and all the women went out after her with timbrels and with dances. And Miriam answered them: "Sing to the Lord, For He has triumphed gloriously! The horse and its rider, He has thrown into the sea!" (Exodus 15:20-21 NKJV)

During Moses' ministry, while everything was running smoothly, it was easy for Miriam and Aaron to sing praises. Though, it is interesting that during times of success, the spirit of disloyalty most often remains silent; it won't reveal itself. Even in troubled times, people tend to tune out negative voices while the ship is making good headway. However, when the wind of progress begins to fade, and the waters are calm, the Jezebel spirit makes its appearance. This spirit begins to "stir the pot" in an atmosphere of uncertainty, or troubled times.

"Then Miriam and Aaron spoke against Moses because of the Ethiopian woman whom he had married; for he had married an Ethiopian woman. So, they said, "Has the Lord indeed spoken only through Moses? Has He not spoken through us also?" And the Lord heard it. (Now the man Moses was very humble, more than all men who were on the face of the earth.)" (Numbers 12:1-3 NKJV)

The Wilderness journey was upon them. They were in the middle of hard times which had become very tiresome; an ideal setting for people to complain. The Israelites were hungry, thirsty, and tired. They were becoming disgruntled and began to question Moses' ability to lead. Then, opposition showed up. The attack didn't come from a foreigner, or from those within the camp, it came from Moses' own siblings.

It is hard to stay loyal and submitted to a family member in leadership when they cannot see beyond what was experienced in childhood. They were witnesses to every shortcoming and every good, or bad, attitude. However, it becomes necessary to discern the difference between the family member and the anointing of the Holy Spirit on that family member. At this point, if they choose to stay connected to the anointing, a change of mindset must take place. It should be understood, there are times to be family, but then there are times when leadership takes precedence over family. With sarcasm, I have heard it said, *"You're supposed to be a Pastor."*

Miriam complained to Aaron, **"Has the Lord indeed spoken only through Moses? Has He not spoken through us also?"** Wow! This statement is the evidence that trouble is brewing; disloyalty has been revealed. Though God can communicate to others in the camp, He chooses to speak with the anointed leaders over them. This helps to ensure a healthy environment for growth and maturity within the church, otherwise, there would be chaos.

It is important to understand that God hears our conversations. He hears them while at the kitchen table or in restaurants. He hears us in our living rooms, in our churches, or in our cities. Even as He heard Miriam and Aaron's conversation about Moses, He hears how we speak out against our Pastors. God does not take it lightly when his people criticize, or judge, the actions of His anointed ones. He did not permit Miriam or Aaron to get away with their criticizing of Moses and were struck with leprosy. It is a true statement, **"And the Lord heard it."** (Numbers 12:13)

"Suddenly the Lord said to Moses, Aaron, and Miriam, "Come out, you three, to the tabernacle of meeting!" So, the three came out. Then the Lord came down in the pillar of cloud and stood in the door of the tabernacle and called Aaron and Miriam. And they both went forward. Then He said, "Hear now My words: If there is a prophet among you, I, the Lord, make Myself known to him in a vision; I speak to him in a dream. Not so with My servant, Moses; He is faithful in all My house. I speak with him face to face, even plainly, and not in dark sayings; And he sees the form of the Lord. Why then were you not afraid to speak against My servant Moses?" (Numbers 12:4-8 NKJV)

Though Miriam and Aaron were Moses' siblings, God was angry with them. He was so angry that Moses prayed that He would heal Miriam so she wouldn't die like a still-born baby in its mother's womb. As a result of his prayer, Miriam had to live outside the camp for seven-days before she could return. This was a harsh lesson that should teach us not to open our mouths against God's anointed Leaders. It is not wise to treat His anointed ones as common.

CLOSING THOUGHT

I believe, "Exposing the Seduction of Disloyalty, will help to bring healing, commitment, and change back to the local church along with its leadership. My goal is to, hopefully, reestablish proper **order** and **government** within the church.

Please use this book as a guide to teach the congregants. The first chapter will give some history surrounding Jezebel and will reveal the purpose of this spirit which is to attack the leadership of our churches, our homes, and our businesses.

Let me caution you, it may go a little deep in the beginning. Stick with it and read it slowly because Jezebel has a connection to history. We will be delving into her origin for the purpose of discovering the root of seduction and disloyalty. We will also learn of the other four insurrectionists and illuminate how they operate. This knowledge will enable you to discern the same characteristics in others. It may also prompt you to stay far away so that you do not fall prey to their seduction.

CHAPTER ONE

WHO IS JEZEBEL?

*J*ezebel was a queen in ancient Israel; her story is told in 1st and 2nd *Kings*. She is introduced as a Phoenician princess who was the daughter of King Ithobaal I, of Sidon; she married King Ahab. In the process of time, she turned Ahab away from the God of the Israelites, along with the inhabitants of Judah, the Jews. Then, Ahab began to worship the Phoenician god, Baal. Because temples of Baal were allowed in Israel, this pagan religion received royal patronage. Jezebel also used her influence, over Ahab, to lead the Hebrews into sin which, in turn, subjected them to tyranny. After she had the prophets of Yahweh killed, the prophet, Elijah, challenged 450 prophets of Baal to a test (1 Kings 18). By exposing Baal as powerless, Elijah was able to have their false prophets slaughtered.[1]

THE MEANING OF THE NAME

Using the vowels traditionally used for the name "Jezebel," the Hebrew form of this name means, **"not exalted."** However, it is highly unlikely her parents would have given her such a name. With different vowels, it can be understood as meaning, **"Where is the prince?"** In fact, early Syrian inscriptions from Ugarit demonstrate that **"The Prince,** equivalent of Hebrew "Zebul," was a popular title for the storm god of the Phoenicians.

The question, **"Where is the prince?"** is even found in Ugaritic literature; an invocation used to call upon the god named to appear and act. In other words, Jezebel was given her name in praise of the chief god

---

[1] From Wikipedia, the free encyclopedia

of her people, Baal, meaning "lord, master."

"Jezebel" is a reinterpretation intended to mock the queen and her god, whom she encouraged Israel to worship. The name, Jezebel, has passed down, through the centuries, as a general name for all wicked women.

In modern usage, the name Jezebel is sometimes used as a synonym for the sexually promiscuous and, sometimes, the controlling woman. This was the case in the title of the 1938 Bette Davis film, "Jezebel"; and, the 1951 Frankie Lane hit, "Jezebel." These films epitomized this fact by the phrase, "Painted Jezebel." In 2 Kings, just before Jezebel is killed, "Painted" refers to her putting on makeup. From a Biblical and/or Christian point of view, a comparison to Jezebel would suggest that a person is either pagan or apostate. Pagan is one **masquerading as a servant of God** who, by manipulation, or seduction, misleads the saints of God into sins of idolatry and sexual immorality. It has also been used to refer to those who challenge the evidence and the belief in God.

In the New Testament, Jezebel's name is used, symbolically, as a **false prophetess who seeks to lure Christians into idolatrous practices.** The story of Jezebel is found in 1 Kings chapters 16, 18, 19, 21, and 2 Kings Chapter 9.

REBELLION IS A FORM OF WITCHCRAFT

Witchcraft is the New Testament ideology that most of us have experienced. Even though the person named Jezebel died, her controlling spirit is alive and functioning well today. She was a person who influenced, or controlled, the kingdom of Israel through the words and the body language of seduction.

God never intended for people to control others, but it happens through seducing words and actions. Even in Church, Pastors should be aware of the temptation to abuse the anointing entrusted to them.

The Jezebel spirit is itself very controlling; it desires to rule and usurp authority for selfish gain. It uses seduction to tempt others to do what they normally would not do. This spirit takes advantage of a person's weakness in order to convince them to be disloyal to the Pastors who are truly in charge. It is important to know where your loyalties lie so as not to fall into this trap.

In the beginning, Satan used the same tactic in the Garden of Eden. Just to be clear, this evil spirit is destroying churches and ministries all over the world.

JEZEBEL DOESN'T WANT TO SIT ON THE THRONE; SHE WANTS TO CONTROL IT!

At first glance, some people who attend church services appear as though they are standing with the ministry and have the Pastor's best interest. However, upon closer inspection, a different story is revealed. Their purpose is to weaken the Pastor's position and gain control for themselves. And, as an insurrectionist, destruction of the Pastor's power, position, and influence is the only objective.

The Jezebel spirit mainly oppresses, or possesses, women causing them to rule over their husbands. It can usually be found operating in homes where the man is in subjection to a bossy woman. In many cases, the man will be submissive and quiet in nature; he will not speak up but will cower down to her control. In public, they act as if they are madly in love, however, it is a mask, or a front. She calls all the shots in private. Thankfully, not all strong women are open doors for this demonic spirit to harass others.

In my opinion, Jezebel causes more damage and creates more dissension than many of the other insurrection spirits within the church. Since Church government has weakened over the last twenty-years, this demon has gotten stronger and gained more control.

What kind of person does Jezebel seek out?

First, it seeks those dissatisfied with life. The Jezebel spirit looks for unhappy individuals lacking joy; they are easy to persuade as well as control. This spirit feeds off the one who always complains, who dislikes everything, and who typically gives negative responses. The prospect of change makes this person nervous.

For years, a previous staff member carried an off-putting, negative attitude; they found the "wrong" in everything. While discussing potential changes, he would inevitably ask the question, *"why is it needed." "It costs too much"* was his answer to spending more money.

On multiple occasions, before church, my staff would warn me of this individual's attitude. "Watch out, Bishop, so and so is in one of their moods." I believe, when a person's presence motivates others to run, that person is a breeding ground for disloyalty. If the contention caused by this spirit is not corrected, it will eventually destroy the ministry.

Also, be wise in the promoting of joyless people. They have an inward problem and have not discovered who they are in Christ. They lack the security of the joy and inner peace capable of keeping them during troublesome times.

Secondly, it seeks those who have a spirit of jealousy. Many times, though I had not made it to the office, this same staff member would call and demand to know where I was, and why I wasn't there. Inevitably, I would get angry. It was not his place to question my comings, or my goings; he was not the boss. I not only hired him, but I wrote and signed his check. It was unfortunate that he neither respected my office nor my position as a man of God. Once I realized he was not trainable, or teachable, I should have fired him. Get this! Recognizing these traits is beneficial when unmasking those who will become disloyal. And, most people who defend their actions, will make excuses as to why they won't change. Their excuses are empty; through Christ Jesus, all people are capable of change.

OLD THINGS PASS AWAY...

*"Now we look inside, and what we see is that anyone united with the Messiah gets **a fresh start** and is **created new**. The old life is gone; a new life burgeons! Look at it! All this comes from the God who settled the relationship between us and him, and then called us to settle our relationships with each other."* (2 Corinthians 5:17-18; The Message Bible)

Look also at this translation:

"Therefore, if anyone is in Christ, he is a new creation; old things have passed away; behold, all things have become new. Now all things are of God, who has reconciled us to Himself through Jesus Christ, and has given us the ministry of reconciliation." (2 Corinthians 5:17-18; NKJV)

Thirdly, it seeks those who have hidden agendas. The Jezebel spirit also seeks out people who serve with one objective, selfish gain. They become self-worshiping, faithful servants of Baal.

WHAT IS BAAL WORSHIP?

What is Baal worship? is a question most believers, in the church, would not be able to answer. And, Bible students are only, generally, aware that the god, **Baal,** is repeatedly mentioned in the scriptures. Because Baal worship, for the most part, is not understood in our churches, I will give a brief history. I will begin with a short passage of scripture in 1 Kings 18.

"And it came to pass, when Ahab saw Elijah, that Ahab said unto him, Art thou he that troubleth Israel?

And he answered, I have not troubled Israel; but thou, and thy father's house, **in that ye have forsaken the commandments of the LORD, and thou hast followed Baalim.***"* (1 Kings 18: 17-18; KJV)

According to this passage, Baal worship became a major religion in the Old Testament. God was incensed with the actions of His people as they began prostrating themselves, in worship, to this foreign god called Baal. Many believe this pagan religion faded into history but, on the contrary, it is active in modern cultures of today. '**Baalim'** is the plural Hebrew word for, "**BAAL, the pagan god of nature and**

fertility."

The Westminster Dictionary of the Bible states,

"... Baal worship apparently had its origin in the belief that every tract of ground owed its productivity to a supernatural being, or Baal, that dwelt there. The farmers probably thought that from Baalim, or fertility gods, of various regions, came the increase of crops, fruit, and cattle. The worship of **Baal** was accompanied with lascivious rites (1 Kings 14:24), the sacrifice of children in the fire by parents (Jeremiah 19:5) and kissing the image (1 Kings 19:18; Hosea 13:2). **Baal** was often associated with the goddess, **Astoreth** (Judges 2:13), and near his altar there was often an **Asherah**. (Judges 6:30; 1 Kings 16:32-33; R.V. – emphasis mine)"

This book is not about sexuality; however, I want to build a case for Baal, the spirit of seduction...

Of the goddess, **Astoreth,** The Westminster Dictionary states,

"... She was the goddess of sexual love, maternity, and fertility. Prostitution, as a religious rite, in the service of this goddess, and under various names, is widely attested. For the benefit of those who preach the Bible, the identification of 'Ashtaroth with Aphrodite is evidence of her sexual character."

"Ashtaroth" (plural of Astoreth). In connection with the plural of Baal, a general designation for the female divinities of the Canaanites, "Asherah", refers to a wooden pole, or mast, which stood at Canaanite places of worship (Exodus 34:13). Originally, it was, perhaps, the trunk of a tree with branches chopped off, and was regarded as the wooden symbol of the goddess Asherah, who, like Ashtoreth, was a type of fertility symbol. It was erected beside the altar of Baal. (Judges 6:25, 28)"

From these quotes, it is apparent that **Baal** and **Ashtaroth** incorporated illegal sexual activity in their worship while Asherah was nothing but a phallic symbol. Lascivious means lewd, lustful, licentious, lecherous, and bawdy. In other words, **Baal worship was accompanied with sinful, sexual acts; behavior expressly forbidden in Jehovah's law**. Now, it is possible to understand how Baal works through the spirit of seduction. The question becomes, "what were those forbidden sexual acts?" Today's culture epitomizes a sex-craved world; it is talked about, written in song, and portrayed in the entertainment field worldwide. As an activity, people are obsessed with sex. Few can doubt the assessment, **"Sex is big business!"** Nevertheless, what does **Most High God** think about modern man's preoccupation with sex? What does His law reveal about sexual matters? Has He given humanity instructions on the discipline of its sexual behaviors?

In today's culture, preaching **Jehovah's law** requires lots of courage.

<u>Adultery</u>: *"Thou shalt not commit adultery."* (Exodus 20:14)

Sexual acts with a person other than your spouse (Leviticus 20:10; Proverbs 6:32; Jeremiah 23:14).

<u>Fornication/Whoredom</u>: *"Do not prostitute thy*

daughter, to cause her to be a whore; lest the land fall to whoredom, and the land become full of wickedness." (Leviticus 19: 29)

"Flee fornication. Every sin that a man doeth is without the body; but he that committeth fornication sinneth against his own body." (1 Corinthians 6: 18)

Sexual acts between unmarried persons for pleasure, or profit.

Homosexuality: *"If a man also lie with mankind, as he lieth with a woman, both of them have committed an abomination: they shall surely be put to death; their blood shall be upon them."* (Leviticus 20: 13)
"But the men of Sodom were wicked and sinners before the LORD exceedingly." (Genesis 13:13)

"And the LORD said, Because the cry of Sodom and Gomorrah is great, and because their sin is very grievous; I will go down now, and see whether they have done altogether according to the cry of it, which is come unto me; and if not, I will know." (Genesis 18:20:21)

In his letter to the Romans, the Apostle Paul wrote of the sin of **homosexuality.** This sin came about as a direct result of men rejecting God's purpose for marriage and procreation. Sex was designed to be between a man, and a woman, within a marriage setting. Its purpose was designed, by the Creator, to fill the earth with other men, and women. However, because men refuse to believe in these basic, biblical truths, homosexuality is becoming normalized in today's society. (Romans 2:18)

WORD OF IMPORTANCE

This is not my opinion; the Bible commands every Christian to represent truth. The fear of persecution is not an excuse for watering down the principles of God's Word. Pastors need to preach boldly, in the Holy Spirit, and proclaim the unadulterated truths of the Bible.

THE DAYS OF NOAH!

In the days of Noah, people were often preoccupied with **eating, drinking** and **sexual activity**. Restraint had been removed and their appetite became their god. For One-hundred and twenty years, Noah preached a message of warning to the people, however, it was to no avail. He was laughed at and referred to as crazy. They believed Noah had no idea what he was talking about. Today could be described in the same way; people are obsessed with **eating, drinking,** and **sexual activity**. However, today, it is fast-tracking to being against the law to condemn any, and all, sexual behavior. Does this mean that Pastor's should be silent? Absolutely Not! Our commission is to warn mankind of the coming judgment against sexual sin, not hide behind a wall of silence.

Jesus warned us in the New Testament

"But as the days of Noah were, so shall also the coming of the Son of man be. For as in the days that were before the flood they were eating and drinking, marrying and giving in marriage, until the day that Noah entered into the ark, and knew not until the flood came, and took them all away; so shall also the

coming of the Son of man be." (Matthew 24:37-39)

"And as it was in the days of Noah, so shall it be also in the days of the Son of man. They did eat, they drank, they married wives, they were given in marriage, until the day that Noah entered into the ark, and the flood came, and destroyed them all." (Luke 17:26-27)

There is, of course, nothing wrong with **eating, drinking,** and **getting married;** people would cease to exist without them. In the New Testament, Jesus revealed that mankind would **become obsessed with gluttony, drunkenness, and a sexual behavior that violates His Divine Law.**

In the Days of Lot

In the days of the patriarch, Lot, a similar situation developed. He lived in the town of Sodom whose name came to represent the homosexual act between two males.

"Likewise, also as it was in the days of Lot; they did eat, they drank, they bought, they sold, they planted, and they built; But the same day that Lot went out of Sodom it rained fire and brimstone from heaven, and destroyed them all. Even thus shall it be in the day when the Son of man is revealed." (Luke 17: 28-30)

Summary

Baal worship is not just a historical phenomenon, in these last days, it is widespread. **Baal worship is the free reign of the carnal nature** which expresses itself through gluttony, drunkenness, and unbiblical sexual acts.

The **Elijah Message** calls people back to the commandments given by **Yahweh,** the Almighty God of Israel; it calls them back to a place of obedience. On the physical level, its message denounces sexual sin. On the spiritual level, it denounces the observance of pagan festivals.

Though a vast number of mankind will continue to worship **Baal**, there will be many **overcomers**; believers who keep the commandments of God. They will have the faith of **Yeshua, the Messiah (Jesus Christ).** In the last days, it is important that every believer be named as the end-time remnant church.

Baal worship is connected to **self-worship**. When you place your desires, your wants, and your life above God's purposes, you have walked through the door of the Baal worshipper. Unfortunately, you are now in a position in which you can be seduced and beguiled by the serpent.

THE SEDUCTION OF WRONG VOICES

"Now the serpent was more cunning than any beast of the field which the Lord God had made. And he said to the woman, "Has God indeed said, 'You shall not eat of every tree of the garden?" And the woman said to the serpent, "We may eat the fruit of the trees of the garden; but of the fruit of the tree which is in the midst of the garden, God has said, 'You shall not eat it, nor shall you touch it, lest you die.'" Then the serpent said to the woman, "You will not surely die.

For God knows that in the day you eat of it your eyes will be opened, and you will be like God, knowing good and evil." So, when the woman saw that the tree was good for food, that it was pleasant to the eyes, and a tree desirable to make one wise, she took of its fruit and ate. She also gave to her husband with her, and he ate. Then the eyes of both of them were opened, and they knew that they were naked; and they sewed fig leaves together and made themselves coverings. And they heard the sound of the Lord God walking in the garden in the cool of the day, and Adam and his wife hid themselves from the presence of the Lord God among the trees of the garden. Then the Lord God called to Adam and said to him, "Where are you?" So he said, "I heard Your voice in the garden, and I was afraid because I was naked; and I hid myself." And He said, "Who told you that you were naked? Have you eaten from the tree of which I commanded you that you should not eat?" Then the man said, "The woman whom You gave to be with me, she gave me of the tree, and I ate." And the Lord God said to the woman, "What is this you have done?" The woman said, "The serpent deceived me, and I ate..." (Genesis 3:1-13, NKJV)

In order to discover truth, you must first reach back into its origin and find out how it all began. By looking way back into Genesis or, the 'beginning,' we can discover how and when Baal first entered the earth to deceive humans.

God's Church in Complete Harmony

First, we should know that God's garden of Eden, was in complete harmony; there was perfect peace with the land, with God, and with man.

Everyday God would come into the Garden and walk with His man. Do not misunderstand, God never left the Garden. He is spirit and He occupies all of creation. However, He had a particular time of day that He met with Adam.

For a while, God and man walked together in unity. How could this be? In the beginning, man was not focused on himself, he was focused on God. He was focused on the eternal purposes of God in the earth. And, when man stayed engaged with what God was doing, then, being human, or mortal beings with weaknesses, did not concern them. Unfortunately, their focus began changing and they started seeing their lives through a dark filter.

I believe the Garden of Eden was a type of the church, and while there was unity to God's vision and plan, they had unbroken communication with Him. Mankind was able to freely walk, and talk, with God. Somehow, God's perfect world became confused and disorderly. A place of peace and security became a place where fear, worry and, deceit intruded upon His creation.

SATAN IS ALWAYS ATTRACTED TO THOSE WHO ARE MOST LIKE HIM.

The serpent was most like the character and nature of Lucifer.

"Now the serpent was more cunning than any beast of the field which the Lord God had made. And he said to the woman..." (Genesis 3:1)

> **"Whoever has your ear has your future..."**

The word *"cunning"* means,

clever. It means marked by or given to artful subtlety and deceptiveness. It is skilled deception, or guile; it is adeptness, in execution, or performance.

What does this cunning, deceptive serpent do? He speaks. Whoever has your ear has your future. So, as soon as Eve gave her ear to the serpent, she lost the battle. She was ensnared the moment she started listening to him. In the blink of an eye, her future was decided by the enemy. The same can happen when we give our attention to people walking in the spirit of dissension.

The serpent gains access by asking questions that distract from the truth. As soon as Eve took her eyes off the God she was connected to, she fell. Why? She became self-absorbed or focused on her own desires. This was the moment that "Self-Image" attached itself to mankind. Now, all of mankind fights this battle.

The serpent told Eve, *"You will not surely die. For God knows that in the day you eat of it your eyes will be opened, and you will be like God, knowing good and evil."* (Gen 3:4-5)

The serpent fed Eve a lie when he told her she would be like God; she was already like God. People who don't understand who they really are will become self-seekers, and self-promoters, rather than God-seekers.

THE SERPENT CAN NOT DESTROY GOD'S CHURCH.

In Genesis, the enemy entered the sanctuary of

Most High God. He wanted to destroy the people who were connected to it; however, this is not true for New Testament believers. In Matthew 16:18, Jesus tells us, *"The gates of Hell shall not prevail against His church."* Thankfully, Satan cannot destroy the church without the help of those who give their ear to wrong voices. He follows the same deceptive tactics as he used in the Garden of Eden. Currently, the church of God is under attack and the spirit of disloyalty can be found sitting in the pews of every Church. It is time to cut off the head of this spirit, Jezebel. And, every insurrectionist who attempts to divide the Kingdom of God should lose their head as well. It is time to declare war over the purposes and intents of every controlling spirit within the Church of God. According to Psalm 21:11, "For they intended evil against you; They devised a plot which they are not able to perform."

CHAPTER TWO

FIVE MOST DAMAGING INSURRECTIONISTS

> *"But there was no one like Ahab who sold himself to do wickedness in the sight of the Lord, because Jezebel his wife stirred him up. And he behaved very abominably in following idols, according to all that the Amorites had done, whom the Lord had cast out before the children of Israel."*
> (1 Kings 21:25-26 NKJV)

That verse brings cold chills down my spine. *"There was no one like Ahab who sold himself to do wickedness in the sight of God."* How did Ahab fall so low? This scripture tells us that *Jezebel, his wife, stirred him up.* One of the main things the enemy does is to send people, into churches, who will stir up division. They are there for the purpose of sabotaging the ministry, the Pastor's family, along with their friendships. And, if possible, abort the destiny of the Church. The Hebrew translation of, *stirred him up,* means to scrub or to trash; it is like a wild growth of weeds or briers placed in the field. It also means to sooth, to prick, or to stimulate which are terms related to seduction. The one who seduces can entice, tempt, lure, persuade, and beguile others. Although the name Jezebel is the most popular name when describing disloyalty, she is not alone. I have discovered at least five additional disloyal personalities.

Five Insurrectionists

Insurrectionists have personalities who are capable of being divisive. They represent demonic personalities that most people encounter during the course of their lives. Even now, one, or more, is probably active in our own lives. Though insurrectionist thoughts may fill a person's mind, that doesn't make them one. However, the problem comes when those thoughts are acted upon; especially for selfish gain. Whether a wolf in sheep's clothing, or the prey of a divisive person, the Bible has the answer. Romans 13:14 states, "Clothe yourselves with the Lord Jesus Christ, and do not think about how to gratify the desires of the flesh." Doing this will help to prevent the anger, jealousy, and disobedience that can arise as a result of an insurrectionist trashing the influence of a Pastor.

WHO ARE THE INSURRECTIONISTS?

- Lucifer (Revelation 12:9)
- Judas (Matthew 27:5)
- Jezebel (1 Kings 21:25)
- Absalom (2 Samuel 18:15)
- Ahithophel (2 Samuel 17:23)

LUCIFER

"Moreover, the word of the Lord came to me, saying, "Son of man, take up a lamentation for the king of Tyre, and say to him, 'Thus says the Lord God:"You were the seal of perfection, Full of wisdom and perfect in beauty. You were in Eden, the garden of God; every precious stone was your covering: The sardius, topaz, and diamond, Beryl, onyx, and jasper, Sapphire, turquoise, and emerald with gold. The workmanship of your timbrels and pipes was prepared for you on the day you were created. "You were the anointed cherub who covers; I established you; You were on the holy mountain of God; You walked back and forth in the midst of fiery stones. You were perfect in your ways from the day you were

created, till iniquity was found in you. "By the abundance of your trading You became filled with violence within..." (Ezekiel 28:11-16 NKJV)

Though this is talking about the King of Tyre, most scholars believe this is really referencing Baal, or Lucifer, who is influencing him. This passage reveals the creation of God's anointed cherub, Lucifer. It briefly describes his purpose and describes him as perfect until iniquity was found in him. After this occurred, he was filled with violence.

At his creation, Lucifer was one of God's Guardian Angels known as an Archangel. The Holy Bible references only three Archangels: **Michael, Gabriel, and Lucifer.** Each had specific positions in heaven prior to Lucifer's fall. Michael was known as a Warring Angel who carried a sword and had power to fight. He was assigned to bring victory to the assignments of God and was the leader over heavenly warfare.

"Then he said to me," Do not fear, Daniel, for from the first day that you set your heart to understand, and to humble yourself before your God, your words were heard; and I have come because of your words. But the prince of the kingdom of Persia withstood me twenty-one days; and behold, **Michael, one of the chief princes,** *came to help me, for I had been left alone there with the kings of Persia. Now I have come to make you understand what will happen to your people in the latter days, for the vision refers to many days yet to come."* (Daniel 10:12-14 NKJV)

Daniel set his heart to hear from God regarding Israel's future, so he prayed. It so happened, God answered immediately, however, it took the angelic forces twenty-one days to get him His answer. Michael, one of the chief princes, was sent in order to help breakthrough the warfare that was taking place against the Prince of Persia. And, after twenty-one days of battle, Daniel received the answer God provided.

Michael was also created to stand watch over the people of Israel.

*"At that time Michael shall stand up, the great prince **who stands watch over the sons of your people**; And there shall be a time of trouble, such as never was since there was a nation, Even to that time..."* (Daniel 12:1 NKJV)

God sent Michael, the archangel, to collect the bones of Moses.

"Yet Michael the archangel, in contending with the devil, when he disputed about the body of Moses, dared not bring against him a reviling accusation, but said, 'The Lord rebuke you!'" (Jude 9-10 NKJV)

The Archangel, Gabriel, was assigned to deliver messages which were sent from the throne of God; he is known, by me, as the *messenger* angel.

"...the man Gabriel, whom I had seen in the vision at the beginning, being caused to fly swiftly, reached me about the time of the evening offering. And he informed me, and talked with me..." (Daniel 9:21-22 NKJV)

"And the angel answered and said to him, "I am Gabriel, who stands in the presence of God, and was

sent to speak to you and bring you these glad tidings." (Luke 1:19 NKJV)

Then, there was the third archangel named, Lucifer.

You were the seal of perfection, Full of "...wisdom and perfect in beauty." (Ezekiel 28:12 NKJV)

Like man, archangels were created with free will. Unfortunately, if sin was found in angels, there was not a redemptive plan to save them from apostasy. They could not be redeemed. This is the situation we have come to understand about Lucifer. He sinned and cannot be redeemed.

"Anything unflawed is an illusion..."

The problem with Lucifer was that he believed he was perfect due to the fact there were no flaws found in him. *"Your heart was lifted up because of your beauty; you corrupted your wisdom for the sake of your splendor..."* (Ezekiel 28:17 NKJV) When God created Lucifer, he was like all the fine and precious jewels on the earth; *"every precious stone was your covering: The sardius, topaz, and diamond, Beryl, onyx, and jasper, Sapphire, turquoise, and emerald with gold."* (Ezekiel 28:13)

With man, God did something different, He made him flawed... **"Anything unflawed is an illusion..."** It is man's flaws, and their weaknesses, that drive them to seek out God. And, the goal of any man should be to attain the Creator's perfection. It is in God's presence that weaknesses die but, to Lucifer, he didn't have any weaknesses. He was an illusion to himself, and to others.

Lucifer was created with the ability to lead the multitudes of Heaven in the worship of God. He was Heaven's choir, and band director, anointed to sing in great harmony.

The Archangel, Lucifer, knew that he was the seal of perfection, without a flaw in him. Therefore, he began to think of himself as equal to God. The Godhead, made up of the Father, the Son, and the Holy Spirit, are three in one, or equal. Because Lucifer was anointed, he believed himself equal to God as well. He began to think he deserved to be worshipped and began to worship himself instead of God. Lucifer starting believing his own deception, his own fan mail. So, *he started talking about his perfection* and was unable to see his own flaws in comparison to God.

Lucifer, the first insurrectionist, is a personality that cannot see his own weaknesses or flaws. His desire is to take the throne, or leadership position, of those over him. Isaiah 14:13 states, *"For you have said in your heart: I will ascend into heaven, I will exalt my throne above the stars of God, and I will sit on the mount of assembly in the recesses of the north."*

Those who are gifted with the same anointings as Lucifer should be aware of falling into the same trap created by pride. Musicians are upfront ministry and can, mistakenly, usurp worship for themselves. Unfortunately, pride in their abilities can cause them to think of themselves as more important, or more needed. They may even develop a mind-set, or attitude, "You can't do this without me." However, God can anoint a rock to worship under the same anointing. The musician is not the center of attention, but the power of God. He is the Source, the Creator of all increase and success...not man! In Church, musical giftings are greatly appreciated, however, those abilities are not the reason we give praise to God. I would rather worship without music rather than allow an insurrectionist to steal what belongs to the Father.

Lucifer ***was***, unknowingly, flawed. He, mistakenly, compared himself to God which left him without the option of redemption; instead, *"he was filled with violence."* (Ezekiel 28:16)

After the creation, God intentionally stayed out of the affairs of man. Genesis 1:28 states, *"Then God blessed them, and God said to them, 'Be fruitful and multiply; fill the earth and subdue it; have dominion over the fish of the sea, over the birds of the air, and over every living thing that moves on the earth."* God handed over all authority to man, however, in order for them to make wise decisions concerning His creation, He would make Himself accessible to them. He would walk with them through the garden of life. It was vital, though, that they stay connected to Him. Otherwise, they would lose the ability to rule in righteousness and their purpose would end up hollow and empty. There is good news though, this emptiness will cause man to seek something better; something deeper; and something, or Someone, with more substance. Someone, like Jesus, with more love, and more joy. As it stands, God is the only, real, source of our joy and peace.

His presence is the only place our weaknesses die.

JUDAS

In my opinion, of the five, Judas is the least divisive. Judas loved Jesus and he willingly sat under His teachings. Judas wanted Jesus to be King over Israel, however, he wanted the Kingdom of God to be established without Jesus dying. He didn't want to wait on God's timing, he wanted to fight the enemy his way. So, in all appearances, Judas was for Jesus.

Those with a Judas spirit, or personality, also love those in leadership. They want to see the ministry ruling, and having dominion, over darkness. They willingly sit under the Pastor's teaching, and they give the appearance of support, but inwardly they are like Judas. They want success to come by their own hands, rather than waiting on God.

> **"Give Judas a rope and he will hang himself..."**

Through dying on the cross, Jesus would win. The Kingdom of God would be established, and it would far outweigh any kingdom that had ever reigned before. However, the Kingdom would rule the spiritual world first. This made Judas angry. Again, he wanted the Kingdom to be established NOW and he was willing to fight to make that happen.

When Judas saw he could not force Jesus to give up His assignment, he became torn between loyalty, and disloyalty. He could not believe Jesus would die before setting up His Kingdom. So, for thirty-pieces of silver, Judas betrayed the Son of Man. Though, after realizing he had betrayed an innocent man, he returned the money, then hung himself. The Judas insurrectionist lacks the understanding of God's purpose in an assignment, therefore, if given a rope, they will hang themselves. Be aware of those individuals who want a ministry's success to come any other way but God's. They will give the appearance of support and will purchase items necessary for the ministry but, then, they will expect everything to be done according to their ideas. When this doesn't happen, they get angry and, by leaving, they betray the ministry.

JEZEBEL

"But there was no one like Ahab who sold himself to do wickedness in the sight of the Lord, because Jezebel his wife stirred him up." (I Kings 21:25)

Again, this verse causes chills to run down my spine. Ahab sold himself, or prostituted himself, to do wickedness before God; he was easily influenced by Jezebel's ability to control and seduce him. Jezebel is an insurrectionist skilled at manipulating circumstances in order to achieve her own goals. She is at the top of her game when it comes to controlling, seducing, or manipulating people. Her eyes, her body language, and even her words reveal a seduction capable of influencing the outcome of any decision. This spirit is a master at causing the other person to believe they have every decision under control. However, in reality, Jezebel has complete control.

Jezebel never sat on a throne nor did she lead from her position as the King's wife. However, her type of spirit hides in the shadows; it hides behind those who are anointed to rule. The serpent, who came to Eve in the Garden of Eden, was possessed by a smooth, talking spirit who rallied for control. He sought to usurp what belonged to Adam; the earth and all it contained. The serpent was able to seize control by asking manipulating questions based on information Eve did not have. He used subtle language, and underlying messages, to seduce her into eating the forbidden fruit. The serpent cunningly swayed Eve's understanding of God's instructions, therefore, he was able to control the outcome. And, as a result, Adam was no longer ruler over God's creation.

"Whoever has your ear has control over your

future."

Discerning the voices that influence your life is vital. If Eve could have known who was asking her the questions, the outcome would have been much different. Adam would have retained the blessing of ownership and he wouldn't have been the recipient of the curse which, immediately, filled the earth. The Word in 1 John 4:1 says, *"Beloved, do not believe every spirit, but test the spirits to see whether they are from God, for many false prophets have gone out into the world."* Don't let the serpents, the Jezebels, deceive you out of your future.

TIME TO BE EXPOSED

One of the most vile, illegitimate, and evil powers, in the church, is an unsanctioned person who declares himself, or herself, to be a prophet, or prophetess; this is breeding ground for the Jezebel spirit. **Be assured, I am not advocating against prophecy, or the prophetic word.** However, apart from the Holy Spirit's involvement, those words come from a controlling spirit. And, it is very unwise to say, "thus saith the Lord" if He hasn't spoken.

For years, I hoped God would expose this spirit within my church. Silently, during our weekly services, I would watch as this spirit would speak "prophetic" words to others while wishing they, themselves, would leave. Unfortunately, the insurrectionist stays in order to gather a following; one who turns to their way of thinking. As hard as those times were, it didn't matter how much I prayed, fasted, or cried to the Lord about this spirit, it would not leave. However, when the crying stopped, I began to understand how necessary it was for me, not God, to confront this demonic influence. It was my responsibility, for God had already given me the authority to trample on this snake. And, the risk of doing nothing involved innocent people getting hurt, deceived, or possibly, spiritually destroyed. If they had been allowed to continue hearing the toxic venom, or words, coming from the insurrectionist, they would eventually have to leave as well. The innocent should not have to suffer for the rebellious acts of the guilty.

SIGNS OF AN ACTIVE JEZEBEL SPIRIT

- An overly powerful woman, married to a weak-willed husband who never stands his ground, or raises the standard in his own house.
- Someone who attempts to gain access to church leadership by ignoring established protocols.
- A person who uses words of flattery in order to gain access. They are ego scratchers who praise you on arrival, then, insult you when they leave.
- Sexual, and sensual, in their actions.
- Overly flirty people who have an agenda.
- People who agree with you, then, question your decisions behind your back.
- People with marital issues.
- Immodestly dressed women.

These are characteristics of a Jezebel spirit; however, they don't always reveal a person to be an insurrectionist. If one of these signs is active, a controlling spirit is able to come through that door. This personality will, mostly, control others through women, but men can fall prey to this as well.

ABSALOM

"After this it happened that Absalom provided himself with chariots and horses, and fifty men to run before him. Now Absalom would rise early and stand beside the way to the gate. So it was, whenever anyone who had a lawsuit came to the king for a decision, that Absalom would call to him and say, "What city are you from?" And he would say, "Your servant is from such and such a tribe of Israel." Then Absalom would say to him, "Look, your case is good and right; but there is no deputy of the king to hear you." Moreover, Absalom would say, "Oh that I were made judge in the land, and everyone who has any suit or cause would come to me; then I would give him justice." And, so it was, whenever anyone came near to bow down to him that he would put out his hand and take him and kiss him. In this manner Absalom acted toward all Israel who came to the king for judgment. So, Absalom stole the hearts of the men of Israel." (2 Samuel 15:1-6 NKJV)

Absalom is the fourth controlling spirit we will be discussing. He was one of King David's sons and became known as *"the most handsome man in all Israel. He cut his hair only once a year, and then only because it was so heavy."* (2 Samuel 14:25, 26). Though he was the King's son, he was not secure in his identity.

> "Never give mercy where God has declared judgment..."

Absalom represents those who are **UNGRATEFUL;** those who are easily offended. This personality possesses an "all about me" attitude who is willing to take what he wants. They seek out opportunities to usurp authority as Absalom did when, *"he would rise early and stand beside the way to the gate."* He did this in order to *"steal the hearts of the men of Israel."* This insurrectionist will listen to the people's complaints then use them as a way to control the ministry as well as leadership.

In his first public act, Absalom took revenge on Amnon, David's eldest son, who had raped his sister, Tamar. Two-years later, during sheep shearing season, Absalom prepared a feast and requested that all his brothers attend. Then, he gave his men instructions stating, *"wait until Amnon gets drunk; then at my signal, kill him."* In horror, David's other sons fled the scene and headed back to Jerusalem. Absalom escaped to his grandfather, Talmai, and lived there for three-years. (2 Samuel 3:3; 13:23-38)

Afterwards, when David had accepted Amnon's death, he desired to see Absalom which was, ultimately, a grave mistake. Love for his son, Absalom, blinded David to the law, *"An eye for an eye and a tooth for a tooth."* The act of revenge required David to have Absalom put to death, but this didn't happen; he was exiled instead. As a result, it brought trouble and division to his kingdom.

During Absalom's exile, David mourned for him and requested that he return to Jerusalem. However, after honoring this request, he was not allowed to see David for two-years. (2 Samuel 14:28) While absent from his father, Absalom began to have aspirations for David's throne. So, he went to Hebron, instigated rebellion against his father and, proclaimed himself King. This conspiracy gained momentum prompting David to flee Jerusalem. Then, Absalom returned to Jerusalem and, without opposition, took the throne. David would not fight Absalom because he was guilty for not carrying out God's law.

THOUGHT: *Watch out for people who want to talk negatively about the ministry rather than talking to the Pastor. My question becomes, "what are their motives?"*

THOUGHT: *Being disobedient to God's commands will position you to lose your rank and your throne.*

"You Can't Complain About What You Tolerate."

The Absalom spirit rests on those who may not always do the talking, but they will most assuredly do the listening. They become garbage cans for the grief of others. Verse 2 says that Absalom would sit at the gate to hear the complaints of the people. Gates, in the Bible, always refer to access. When Jacob laid his head on a stone and fell asleep, he dreamed of angels ascending and descending. He said, *"I have found the gate of Heaven."* He was actually saying, "I have found Heaven's access."

The gate called, Beautiful, was a place of access in the city of Israel. And, in chapter three of Acts, a lame man was daily laid at this gate. He was about to meet Peter and John who, through Jesus Christ, would change his life forever; he was destined to walk again.

Absalom positioned himself along the way to the gate in order to persuade the men of Israel to follow him. Why? Because he wanted to be King instead of his father, David. Just as Absalom listened to the complaints of the people, there are people today who do the same thing in our churches; they sit at the back of the church or stand at the entrance and listen. The Absalom spirit is, usually, a person who has been wounded, and rejected, as a result of a trespass. Instead of allowing the wound to heal, they begin searching for the acceptance of others. Then, the pain of rejection prevents the restoration of access into the presence of the established leadership.

Instead of encouraging the wounded to maintain a good standing with the King, this spirit will only sympathize with those who are hurting. ***"Then Absalom would say to him, "Look, your case is good and right; but there is no deputy of the king to hear you."*** (2 Samuel 15:3) This type of approach can cause the wounded individual to seek acceptance from other people. Allow me to extend some caution, it is important to stay in covenant with the KING. In church, it is just as important to stay connected to your, God ordained, ministry leaders.

"...Absalom stole the hearts of the men of Israel." (2 Samuel 15:6)

This spirit goes about stealing the hearts of the people. And, in this scripture, heart means the *mind*. So, Absalom became a "mind stealer." He set out to change the minds of the people in order to alter their belief in David. Eventually, the people began to believe that Absalom was the King of Israel.

- *Your mind bosses your emotions;*
- *Your emotions decide your feelings; and,*
- *Your feelings decide what you connect to.*

The Absalom spirit usually leaves the church in order to start his own ministry. However, it is not because God ordained his departure, it is because he would not sit under the leadership of a Pastor. These individuals would rather meet in their living rooms than submit to a "called" man of God.

CHARACTER OF THE ABSALOM SPIRIT

Phony Compassion

Do not be deceived by Absalom's outward appearance of compassion; this spirit acts out of his own self-interests. And, he is very aware that man is capable of deciding his own wealth and position in life. So, his compassion is directly connected to his ambition, not because he has a heart for the people. Compassionless people fill our congregations; however, though they act caring, it is only an appearance. In reality, their main purpose is to fulfill a predetermined agenda. Absalom also employs gossip and flattery in order to accomplish his goals. Gossip is idle talk or rumor, especially about the personal or private affairs of others. And, flattery is to praise or compliment insincerely, or excessively. (Dictionary.com)

A Stealthy Connection

Be very cautious of people who want to meet in secret; on the phone or, in person, away from the Pastor. People operating rebelliously will always attempt to pull others to their side. And, they can be quite subtle, cunning, and ingenious in those attempts. Unfortunately, the people who lack discernment will miss what's actually happening and get caught up in the confusion. They will become offended with the Pastor even though, previously, they had no reason to be mad. Absalom's are gifted at manipulation. In the end, they cause the misled congregant to become disloyal, then, in God's eyes, are guilty of treason. As a warning, when this spirit is finished with you, it will throw you under the bus. It will sacrifice you for its own gain.

It is wise to guard your heart and not allow yourself to become discontented. If one person is discontented, it will draw others as well. Then, the need for other people to agree with a perceived wound intensifies. Also, avoid rebellious individuals who create division in order to benefit their cause. The spirit of rebellion hates correction; therefore, it will attempt to destroy the one who did the correcting. They have a vindictive attitude. The good news, a rebellious mindset can be exposed with correction.

A Cunning Contention

Cunning means *clever, deceiving, shrewd.* People with an Absalom spirit will try to take matters into their own hands rather than seeking instructions from the Pastor. Someone, with this spirit, believes he is above correction and that rules are meant to be broken. He believes the end justifies the means. Because he has no fear of God, he exalts himself and believes he is better than, and knows more than, leadership.

BREEDING GROUND FOR THE ABSALOM SPIRIT TO GROW (2 Samuel Chapters 13 – 15)

- Offense, hatred, un-forgiveness and bitterness.
- A justifiable, or exaggerated, distrust and resentment of one's authority.
- A basic independence, and self-dependence, as it pertains to honest communication, problem solving, sharing of honest feelings, needs,

wants, etc.
- It is rooted in camouflaged bitterness, unresolved disappointments, fear, anger, impotence, etc.
- It is rooted in irrational secrets that appear, totally, rational to the "Absalom."
- It is rooted in hidden agendas, hidden strategies and hidden alliances. **Key word is hidden.**
- It is rooted in hidden contempt, hatred and revenge of authority along with those under authority.
- It is rooted in pride.
- It is rooted in rebellion and, if allowed to grow, will become unquenchable.
- It is rooted in a deep-seated desire to be close to, next to, or in the place of favor with the one in authority; howbeit, not with a pure heart.
- It is rooted in impressing, and stealing, the hearts of the people who are under authority. Their hope is to, eventually, "dethrone" and replace the one in authority.

MANIFESTATIONS OF THE ABSALOM SPIRIT

- An Absalom spirit will manifest through an attitude of self-promotion. It is focused on what it can get, not on who they serve.
- An Absalom spirit will carefully manifest itself through a constructed, and projected, self-image designed to impress. This person enjoys his work being seen by others; however, in private, he is lazy. Whether in front of the Pastor, or in public, he will give the impression that he is doing all the work. And, as he climbs the ladder of success, he is quick to inform people of his accomplishments while

discrediting others. Though he may appear to be humble, loyal, and caring, I can assure you, he is not.

- An Absalom spirit will manifest through manipulation and loves to exert control over others. This spirit forces its agenda to override the current standards of the organization.

- An Absalom spirit will manifest through selfish ambition disguised as service to others.

- An Absalom spirit will manifest through divisiveness, antagonism, and negative criticism of those in authority; it does this in order to promote self. He will, smugly, sit in the enemy's presence discussing those in leadership.

- An Absalom spirit will manifest through rebellion. In the end, no matter what is said, or done, this person will rebel.

- An Absalom spirit will manifest through false humility.

- An Absalom spirit will manifest through thievery; it will steal the heart, and loyalty, of the people from true leadership. This happens because it acts as though it cares more for the people than the Pastor.

- An Absalom spirit will manifest through treachery. It discusses all the leadership's weaknesses in order to expose them.

- An Absalom spirit will manifest through subtle

seduction.

- An Absalom spirit will manifest through religious hypocrisy and hype. While offering his sacrifice, he gives for show rather than in support of the house's vision. He appears supportive, but is really dangerous to the church.

- An Absalom spirit is ungrateful. Even though David spared his life from judgment and punishment, Absalom became angry because he wanted his father's throne. Be wary of people who are not thankful.

- Absalom judges everyone behind closed doors, but gives the opposite impression to their face.

LIES THE ABSALOM SPIRIT BELIEVES

- Authority is not to be trusted.
- Authority is incompetent.
- Believes, "I know the right way to handle this."
- I am as skilled, and as anointed, as the Pastor.
- God speaks to all, not just the Pastor.

WHY THIS SPIRIT IS DIFFCULT TO DEAL WITH

- Through relationship, people are emotionally attached to this spirit.
- Absalom is nice, lovable, good looking and popular. Everyone loved Absalom, especially, King David; people want to connect with him. Because this spirit is good at deception, it is hard to distinguish his true nature.

- To this personality, it is not Christ-like, or loving, for a Pastor to correct them. However, the best solution is to cut them off. King David invited trouble into his Kingdom by allowing Absalom to return.

    o *Many times, those who operate in an Absalom Spirit will, out of rebellion, leave a church but want to stay connected through fellowship.* Their reasoning, *"Even if we are not in the same church, we are still part of the kingdom of God."*

    o Though this logic sounds good, it is not. Their true motives are discerned by their history and the divisions they caused; to influence and manipulate.

- The Church leadership appears paranoid and fearful if they attempt to discuss these issues with other counsel.

SIGNS OF AN ABSALOM IN YOUR LIFE

- *They seek an audience.* "Now Absalom would rise early and stand beside the way to the gate. So it was, whenever anyone who had a lawsuit came to the king for a decision, that Absalom would call to him and say, "What city are you from?" And he would say, "Your servant is from such and such a tribe of Israel." (2 Samuel 15:2)
- *Love, kindness and favor are their tools. Who can resist that?* They are not committed, nor can they be corrected. And, they

only serve to shape a belief system that is against the church rather than for it.

- ***Absalom appears concerned but uses false kindness in order to steal the hearts of those who are connected to leadership.*** Watch out for people who would befriend those closest to the Pastor. Their purpose is to gain information to use against them.
- ***Use words of flattery such as:*** *"You are special to me." "I love you more than the Pastor does." "Even if the Pastor doesn't, I will spend quality time with you."*
- ***Gives special treatment.*** He begins giving coffee, tea, fellowship, trips, gifts, and favors to those who can, potentially, help him achieve his goals. Most everyone enjoys being treated special; however, in the future they are reminded of the gifts they were given. Absalom's gifts come with a price.
- ***His attitude communicates that nothing coming from the Pastor, or leadership, is ever good enough; He believes he can do it better.*** Even if most of Absalom's ideas are implemented, they will never be good enough. Fault will always be found.
- ***Concerning leadership, they plant doubt in the minds of the followers.*** They will find fault in areas not related to spiritual qualifications. And, they turn minor issues into major ones.
- ***They always have a hidden agenda.*** Absalom's motives for the throne were not known until it was too late. Whereas, people knew where they stood with Jezebel and Korah, they didn't with Absalom because he was

sneaky; he did everything behind David's back.
- ***This spirit will tell you what you want to hear, not the truth you need to hear.*** A Pastor's job is to speak the truth in love. Sometimes, truth hurts and requires the person to change, but it is always for their good.
- ***They will, eventually, reveal themselves through open rebellion, disloyalty, and causing of division.***

As you become aware of an Absalom, it is a good idea to swiftly move away from their influence. **Tell your pastor immediately**! If that connection is not broken, the potential of falling increases dramatically. Exposing this spirit is the only cure from its venom.

AHITHOPHEL

"For it is not an enemy who reproaches me; Then I could bear it. Nor is it one who hates me who has exalted himself against me; Then I could hide from him. But it was you, a man my equal, My companion and my acquaintance. We took sweet counsel together, and walked to the house of God in the throng. Let death seize them; Let them go down alive into hell, For, wickedness is in their dwellings and among them. As for me, I will call upon God, And the Lord shall save me. Evening and morning and at noon I will pray, and cry aloud, And He shall hear my voice. He has redeemed my soul in peace from the battle that was against me, For, there were many against me. God will hear, and afflict them, Even He who abides from of old. Because they do not change, Therefore, they do not fear God." (Psalms 55:12-19 NKJV)

Ahithophel was the royal counselor to King David (1 Chronicles 27:33 NKJV); his counsel was regarded as highly as if someone had sought out the word of God. In Psalm 55, David states, "Who never missed your counsel." According to this, Ahithophel had a good record of giving the right counsel. He made up for what David lacked in political conversation. They were friends until he betrayed David by siding with his son, or enemy, Absalom.

"Now the advice of Ahithophel, which he gave in those days, was as if one had inquired at the oracle of God. So was all the advice of Ahithophel..." (2 Samuel 16:23 NKJV)

David was a man of war and he knew how to strategize in order to win in battle. However, in times of peace, David was as a fish out of water. So, he depended on Ahithophel's wise counsel. As time passed, he abandoned David in order to support Absalom in his rebellion against the throne. Ahithophel became the counselor to Absalom; however, the people did not follow his advice. Therefore, he hung himself. Ahithophel exalted himself against David causing him tremendous pain and anguish. Regardless of this, David would not fight against a man anointed by God.

"It's not my enemy who reproaches me; Then, I could bear it! Fight it! God it is not one who hates me who has exalted himself against me; then I would, or could hide from him. But it was you, Ahithophel, a man of my equal, my friend, my acquaintance. We took sweet counsel together; we walked to the house of God together. Oh God! Let death seize me, or them. I can't fight this man, who never missed your

counsel." (Psalm 55:12-16)

Before you start hating Ahithophel for his defection, listen to the rest of the story. Ask yourself, "Why would a once loyal, and close, confidant turn from David to the enemy?"

"It happened in the spring of the year, at the time when kings go out to battle, that David sent Joab and his servants with him, and all Israel; and they destroyed the people of Ammon and besieged Rabbah. But David remained at Jerusalem." (2 Samuel 11:1 NKJV)

It was the season when kings go out to battle but, instead of going, as was the custom, David stayed home. As a result of not being where he was supposed to be, *"David arose from his bed and walked on the roof of the king's house. And from the roof he saw a woman bathing, and the woman was very beautiful to behold. So, David sent and inquired about the woman. And someone said, 'Is this not Bathsheba, the daughter of Eliam, the wife of Uriah the Hittite?'"* (2 Samuel 11:2-3 NKJV) Uriah, Bathsheba's husband, was among the troops sent to war. After David's inquiry, *"David sent messengers, and took her; and she came to him, and he lay with her, for she was cleansed from her impurity; and she returned to her house. And the woman conceived; so, she sent and told David, and said, 'I am with child.'"* (2 Samuel 11:4-5) Afterwards, David began plotting how to rectify the mess he had created; how to cover his sin.

David sent word for Uriah to return from the battlefield in order to ascertain how the war was prospering. Then, with a gift of food, he sent Uriah home hoping Bathsheba would lay with him. However, as a devoted servant, Uriah did not go to his house, but slept at the door of the king's house. After another attempt at tricking Uriah to lay with his wife, David orchestrated a plot that caused Uriah to be killed on the battlefield.

Now we have to ask ourselves, "How does Uriah, a Hittite, become an officer in the king's army?" As it turns out, Bathsheba was Ahithophel's granddaughter who was married to Uriah. Therefore, Uriah was promoted, by David, due to his connection with Ahithophel. And, because David schemed to have his granddaughter's husband murdered, Ahithophel chose to side with Absalom.

Imagine the questions Ahithophel had: *"Though David could have had any woman he wanted, "Why did you lay with my granddaughter?" "David, we were friends. We ate together... We worshipped together... How could you have done this to my family?"*

At this point, it is not as easy to be mad at Ahithophel for betraying David. Instead, the opposite is now the case; we are a little angry with David. How could this have happened between friends?

Ahithophel defected from David's camp and joined Absalom's where he began to lay out plans to capture the king. To David, the worst part was knowing, "God was angry with him as well." While prostrate before the Lord, he began crying out, *"God if he comes, I will not fight him. I will not touch what you've anointed."* However, Ahithophel was plotting, with Absalom, how they would destroy David, the king.

"And Ahithophel said to Absalom, "Go into your father's concubines, whom he has left to keep the house; and all Israel will hear that you are abhorred by your father. Then the hands of all who are with

you will be strong." So, they pitched a tent for Absalom on the top of the house, and Absalom went in to his father's concubines in the sight of all Israel. Now the advice of Ahithophel, which he gave in those days, was as if one had inquired at the oracle of God. So was all the advice of Ahithophel both with David and with Absalom. Moreover, Ahithophel said to Absalom, "Now let me choose twelve thousand men, and I will arise and pursue David tonight. **I will come upon him while he is weary and weak, and make him afraid. And all the people who are with him will flee, and I will strike only the king.** *Then I will bring back all the people to you. When all return except the man whom you seek, all the people will be at peace." And the saying pleased Absalom and all the elders of Israel."* (2 Samuel 16:21-23 and 2 Samuel 17:1-4 NKJV)

Notice Ahithophel says, *"Let me strike only the king."* David was wrong for having Uriah killed on the battlefield, God would judge him for that, however, He would not allow him to be judged by Ahithophel nor those under his leadership. Though Ahithophel had cause to be mad, even angry, he had no right to raise his hand, or his mouth, against God's anointed King; a major problem with this spirit. Now, the church has begun to believe it has the right to attack God's anointed men and women as well. They do this by exposing their flaws and weaknesses. But, Psalm 105:15 states, *"Touch not mine anointed, and do my prophets no harm."* Clearly, His anointed ones are off limits to the church's attacks.

> **"Never touch a Man of God while he is in transition."**

What happened to Ahithophel?

"Now when Ahithophel saw that his advice was not followed, he saddled a donkey, and arose and went home to his house, to his city. Then he put his household in order, and hanged himself, and died; and he was buried in his father's tomb." (2 Samuel 17:23 NKJV)

Ahithophel hung himself after he realized no one was following his advice. Though he knew God had not given him authority to harm David, his anger had gotten the best of him. Unfortunately, there is a tremendous price to pay when people begin taking someone else's judgment into their own hands. In the end, the scripture, *"Judge not lest you be judged,"* became a reality for Ahithophel.

For anyone who has attempted to follow in Ahithophel's steps, repentance is the only option. Do not hesitate in turning to God for a clean slate; this is one of God's greatest gifts to mankind. And, the sin of Ahithophel, if it is not repented of, can destroy your entire house. Remember, there is no justification for harming God's anointed ones.

In the Gospel of John, after Jesus was raised from the dead, Mary was seen at the tomb of Jesus' burial. On arrival, she noticed the stone which had been covering the tomb, was rolled away. The burial site was now open and Mary saw Jesus standing at its entrance, however, she assumed she was seeing the gardener. She did not recognize her Master, or Teacher, even though she had had close fellowship with Him. So, how could Mary have mistaken Jesus for someone else?

Jesus was no longer the pre-resurrected Jesus. And, He was also preparing to ascend to His place at the right hand of the Father. Though Mary did not recognize His appearance, she did, however, recognize his voice. When Jesus spoke her name, *"Mary,"* she immediately knew who He was. Why? Because, as she sat under His teachings, she became familiar with His voice. Afterwards, she was able to proclaim, *"Master, Teacher,"* while reaching out to touch Him. However, Jesus stopped her by saying, *"Mary don't touch me. I have not yet made full change (or transition). I am not the man I was; however, I am not the man I'm yet supposed to be."* So, never touch a man or woman of God while they are in transition! It could hinder the greatest change in their life, and, in yours. Then, after ascending to God, Jesus returned to inform the disciples, and the church, of their victory over life, death, and the enemy.

Many times, I have seen Pastors begin to act, walk, and talk differently while those within their congregations noticed the changes. People would make remarks such as, *"You're not the same, you act differently"; "You don't talk the same";* and, *"I liked you better before."* These statements come from a lack of understanding. In order for the congregation to grow, the Pastor must change, or he must be different. It needs to be said again; **do not touch a man or woman of God while in transition.** Though it is uncomfortable, stay connected and allow him room to make the necessary changes. Afterwards, when you enter the next season, you will not be disappointed.

WHERE HAS THE POWER GONE?

As I look at today's local church, my spirit is heavy. Unfortunately, the average church attendee will not last more than five years; this is concerning to me. There was a time, no matter what, when people were committed. Now, people are easily uprooted and seem to be on an endless journey to find a church that will stimulate, or tickle, their ear. However, instead of stimulation, cultivation is needed in order to make Christians more powerful. It would also enable them to walk in more freedom and love rather than in bitterness and anger. Un-forgiveness and anger can open doors for the insurrection spirit to take root, then, move a person into disloyalty.

In Isaiah and Mark, Jesus tells us to do good, seek justice, rebuke the oppressor, defend the fatherless, plead for the widow, heal the sick, and cast out demons. (Isaiah 1:17 and Mark 16:17-18) Instead, it seems most churches, along with their people, are *anemic, spiritually impotent,* and in *bondage.* Of course, I am not speaking of all churches, only those where the church organization is more powerful than the people it serves. Many churches have the mind-set of holding down the fort while awaiting Jesus' return, rather than, of learning how to take back what belongs to Him. In reality, they are not holding down anything; this is, in part, because most churches are full of hurting, broken, and unchanged people. They are missing the victorious life and, instead, are living in the wounds of the past. It is important to note, every human being has a past that contains multiple, traumatic, events which gave birth to seasons of pain. However, we can learn to use these seasons, for our advantage, by embracing where we came from rather than living in the pain of the past.

> **"Anything Uncontested Will Flourish."**

"Behold, I give you authority to trample on serpents and scorpions, and over all the power of the

enemy, and nothing shall by any means hurt you." (Luke 10:19 NKJV)

That means, unless people give it permission, the past no longer has power to harm. And, *"Jesus gave the disciples (the church), power over unclean spirits, to cast them out, and to heal all kinds of sickness and all kinds of disease."* (Matthew 10:1 NKJV) The church has been given power, and authority, to walk free from all controlling spirits. So, could it be, many are not, actually, following Jesus, therefore, don't have the spiritual aptitude to be set free. Or, do they lack power because they criticize, backbite, fight, complain, and rebel? Or, they doubt and don't believe God. First John 5:4 states, *"whatever is born of God overcomes the world. And this is the victory that overcomes the world even **our faith**."* So, our first act of overcoming was when we accepted Jesus Christ as our Lord and Savior. Then, by exercising the faith He has already given us, we can have victory over everything else. For, *"God is able to do exceedingly abundantly above all that we ask or think."* (Ephesians 3:20).

Undoubtedly, many problems within the church are due to leadership tolerating, instead of, confronting the issues at hand; and, anything uncontested flourishes. The Bible gives clear instructions on how to deal with unwanted spiritual attacks. It is time for every believer to stand up, in authority, in order to overcome every disloyal spirit.

CHAPTER THREE

CONFRONTING THE SPIRIT OF DISLOYALTY

BINDING TOGETHER

The first, and most deadly, weapon of disloyalty is exposure; it is a must in order to confront and dismantle the work of this insurrectionist. It helps when Pastors inform each other when a person, who is known to be disloyal, leaves their church. Making them aware is beneficial in preventing them from joining a church in order to divide the sheep from the Pastor.

If you have been caught in the web of a disloyal person, repent and cut off the relationship immediately; God will forgive you. Refuse to sit in meetings with those who, continuously, talk about, criticize, or exalt themselves above the Pastor. It is important to stay away from, or run from, those who are demonically driven for the advancement of hell. However, don't just stay away from disloyal people, expose them; disloyalty is the meanest, and hardest, of the insurrectionists to expose.

Also, it is not wise to make friends with this type of spirit, nor with those influenced by it. In most cases, they are unreachable and unwilling to see themselves as part of the problem, or the problem itself.

Years ago, some women started a prayer group in my church. They would meet in the sanctuary and, supposedly, pray for me, my family, and the vision of the church. Though, this went on for years, it did not sit well with me. I began seeing how they disrespected their husbands by exerting too much authority; I also saw how they were resistant to correction. Then, I started questioning the motives of the intercessory prayer group. So, one night, I decided to observe what was happening in those meetings. I sat at the back of the sanctuary and discovered there was very little, true, prayer happening. However, there was a lot of discussion regarding what God was saying about the church, the staff, and the ministry. The intercessory prayer leader would orchestrate and lead the lengthy conversation, then, the praying would start. To me, it was not normal. It was loud and crazy, or super spiritual, with screaming in tongues and prophesying to one another. Afterwards, the leader expressed that this was a typical prayer session. It was not a good experience; I left with my heart pumping, unusually, fast. I began thinking they were there with their own agenda so, I began studying on the Jezebel spirit.

Soon after completing the study, I decided to sit in on another prayer session. Instead of allowing them to speak on the things God was showing them, I spoke up and said, *"I don't want the group to talk about what the Lord is saying to the intercessors; however, I do want to talk about what the Lord is teaching me."* So, I taught them about the "**JEZEBEL SPIRIT**," or, the spirit of control. Let me tell you, I was freaking out. The spirit of the Lord fell on the words being spoken which caused some of the women to have horrified expressions. Right in front of my eyes, it actually appeared as though demons were looking back at me. The women became agitated and restless; they even got angry when I announced presenting this series to the church. When the prayer meeting ended, one of the ladies stated, *"Please don't teach on that subject."* After asking "why," she said, *"Because, every time a preacher talks about that, I have to leave the church."* WOW! Can you believe that? Needless to say, I shut down the prayer group. I realized the enemy was using their group to gain control over this ministry; unfortunately, it took years to overcome its effects.

Because I allowed this to continue, it nearly cost

me everything. As it stands, one of my greatest weaknesses has been walking with the wrong people when I should have let them go. And, my need to fix people has, at times, placed me in unnecessary circumstances.

"Beware of false prophets, who come to you in sheep's clothing, but inwardly they are ravenous wolves. You will know them by their fruits. Do men gather grapes from thornbushes or figs from thistles? Even so, every good tree bears good fruit, but a bad tree bears bad fruit. A good tree cannot bear bad fruit, nor can a bad tree bear good fruit. Every tree that does not bear good fruit is cut down and thrown into the fire. Therefore, by their fruits you will know them." (Matthew 7:15-20 NKJV)

"And have no fellowship with the unfruitful works of darkness, but rather expose them. For it is shameful even to speak of those things, which are done by them in secret. But all things that are exposed are made manifest by the light, for whatever makes manifest is light." (Ephesians 5:11-14 NKJV)

ALONE, THE MAN OF GOD DOES NOT POSSESS THE POWER TO CONQUER THIS DEMON!

Wrestling control, from those who sit in the pews of our churches, will take a team effort. And, in order to win, it is necessary that every individual be in covenant with the one in the pulpit. God will reward those who are loyal to His chosen mouthpiece but, in the end, He will punish those who are disloyal.

GOD CHOOSES WHO TO SPEAK THROUGH

When God speaks, who does He sound like? What does He sound like? During a church gathering, God generally speaks through those He has placed as head of the house. And, when God speaks to other individuals of the house, there are leaders who are able to confirm whether the word was from Him, or not. This is not taught in most churches, especially in the United States. However, in the Word of God, it is the Lord who speaks to the Prophet, the Deliverer, or the Apostle; then, they relay His message to the people. A congregation is led, by God, through His chosen ones. The book of Numbers gives several examples:

- Numbers chapter one... **"Now the Lord spoke to Moses..."**
- Numbers chapter two... **"And the Lord spoke to Moses and Aaron..."**
- Numbers chapter three... **"The Lord spoke with Moses..."**
- Numbers chapter four.... **"Then the Lord spoke to Moses and Aaron saying..."**
- Numbers chapter five... **"And the Lord spoke to Moses, saying...."**
- Numbers chapter six... **"Then the Lord spoke to Moses saying..."**
- Numbers chapter seven... **"Then the Lord spoke to Moses, saying..."**
- Numbers chapter eight... **"And the Lord spoke to Moses, saying..."**
- Numbers chapter nine... **"Now the Lord spoke to Moses in the wilderness of Sinai..."**
- Numbers chapter ten... **"And the Lord spoke to Moses, saying..."**

However, notice what happens when the people involved themselves in God's process of government.

*"**Now when the people complained**, it displeased the Lord; for the Lord heard it, and His anger was aroused. So, the fire of the Lord burned among them, and consumed some in the outskirts of the camp."* (Numbers 11:1 NKJV)

In Numbers chapter 12, Miriam and Aaron spoke against Moses; and, the Lord, punished them.

"Then Miriam and Aaron spoke against Moses because of the Ethiopian woman whom he had married; for he had married an Ethiopian woman. So, they said, "Has the Lord indeed spoken only through Moses? Has He not spoken through us also?" And the Lord heard it." (Numbers 12:1-2 NKJV)

"Suddenly the Lord said to Moses, Aaron, and Miriam, "Come out, you three, to the tabernacle of meeting!" So, the three came out. Then the Lord came down in the pillar of cloud and stood in the door of the tabernacle, and called Aaron and Miriam. And they both went forward. Then He said, 'Hear now My words: If there is a prophet among you, I, the Lord, make Myself known to him in a vision; I speak to him in a dream. Not so with My servant Moses; He is faithful in all My house. I speak with him face to face, Even, plainly, and not in dark sayings; And he sees the form of the Lord. Why then were you not afraid to speak against My servant Moses?" So, the anger of the Lord was aroused against them, and He departed. And when the cloud departed from above the tabernacle, suddenly Miriam became leprous, as

white as snow. Then Aaron turned toward Miriam, and there she was, a leper. So, Aaron said to Moses, "Oh, my lord! Please do not lay this sin on us, in which we have done foolishly and in which we have sinned. Please do not let her be as one dead, whose flesh is half consumed when he comes out of his mother's womb!" So, Moses cried out to the Lord, saying, "Please heal her, O God, I pray!" Then the Lord said to Moses, "If her father had but spit in her face, would she not be shamed seven days? Let her be shut out of the camp seven days, and afterward she may be received again." So, Miriam was shut out of the camp seven days, and the people did not journey till Miriam was brought in again. And afterward the people moved from Hazeroth and camped in the Wilderness of Paran." (Numbers 12:4-16 NKJV)

In this passage, God revealed that Moses was the one He had chosen to speak "face to face" with. And, as a result of Aaron and Miriam speaking against Moses, Miriam contracted leprosy. Moses interceded for her healing, then, was kept outside of camp for seven days. This took place, once again, after the people began to complain. This angered God and He caused His fire to burn among the Israelites; many were consumed outside the camp.

Numbers, chapter 13, states, *"And God spoke to Moses."* So, when Moses speaks, it is as though they are hearing the voice of God. It is the same with the anointed man, or woman, of God today; they speak and the people hear from God.

The Jezebel spirit seduces through words. When people give their ear to this spirit, it can, potentially, decide their future and whether, or not, their church will survive. If you are not yet convinced, in 1 Samuel 2, Hannah was a barren woman; she prayed, fasted, then made a covenant with God. She basically said, if God would give her a son, she would give the child back to Him to be trained for ministry. God heard her prayers, agreed to the covenant, and gave her a son; she named him Samuel. After he was weaned, Hannah returned him to the temple to be raised, and trained, under Eli, the High Priest.

"But Samuel ministered before the Lord, even as a child, wearing a linen ephod." (1 Samuel 2:18 NKJV)

"Now the boy, Samuel, ministered to the Lord before Eli. And the word of the Lord was rare in those days; there was no widespread revelation. And it came to pass at that time, while Eli was lying down in his place, and when his eyes had begun to grow so dim that he could not see, and before the lamp of God went out in the tabernacle of the Lord where the ark of God was, and while Samuel was lying down, that the Lord called Samuel. And he answered, "Here I am!" So, he ran to Eli and said, "Here I am, for you called me." And he said, "I did not call; lie down again." And he went and lay down. Then the Lord called yet again, "Samuel!" So, Samuel arose and went to Eli, and said, "Here I am, for you called me." He answered, "I did not call, my son; lie down again."

At this point, Samuel did not know the Lord, nor had the word of the Lord been revealed to him.

And the Lord called Samuel again the third time. So, he arose and went to Eli, and said, "Here I am, for you did call me." **Then, Eli perceived that the**

***Lord had called the boy**. Therefore, Eli said to Samuel, "Go, lie down; and it shall be, if He calls you, that you must say, 'Speak, Lord, for your servant hears.'" So, Samuel went and lay down in his place. Now, the Lord came and stood and called as at other times, "Samuel! Samuel!" And Samuel answered, "Speak, for your servant hears." **<u>Then the Lord said to Samuel</u>**...*" (1 Samuel 3:1-11 NKJV)

According to this scripture, and previous ones, God calls, He anoints, and they become His mouthpiece. The Old Testament has given us this example, and today, it has not changed. He still calls, anoints, and people become His voice in the land.

SAMUEL'S SEASON WAS ABOUT TO CHANGE!

While Samuel was sleeping, God called for him by name. He assumed it was Eli and went to him; however, he was sent back to bed because he wasn't the one who called him. After the third occurrence, Eli realized it was God calling for Samuel. Why did he assume it was Eli? In part, it is due to Eli being the High Priest, or the vessel that God was speaking through at that time. Again, people are led by God, through His chosen mouthpiece; the anointed man, or woman, appointed as Pastor of the house.

After Eli perceived it was, in fact, God calling the boy, he gave Samuel instructions for the next time He would call. Then, when God came, Samuel heard His voice and responded. This is the pattern... the example. Be wary of the voices who attempt to speak to you about your future, good or bad. If they don't line up with the pattern, it would be wise to ignore them. If your Pastor is truly called, and anointed by God, don't be seduced into listening to any other voice. The Jezebel spirit is capable of leading people down the road of destruction.

MEMBERSHIP MUST EXPOSE AND DESTROY THIS SPIRIT

For the church to be able to destroy the Jezebel spirit, they first need to be equipped in order to discern its activity. Then, they need to be empowered so they can stand and fight. In his day, Elijah, in the Old Testament, was anointed to take down Jezebel. He, as a Prophet of God, was no joke; for, no one could stand against his power or his prophecies. He truly was one of God's most anointed Prophets. He set up a contest between the Lord, and Baal, in order for the people to recognize the one true God; and, reject Baal. After Ahab's prophets did all they could do to get Baal to answer, Elijah called upon the Lord. God answered by fire, burning up the water-soaked sacrifice. Afterwards, Elijah killed all the prophets of Baal, then, he prayed for the three-year drought to end. When Ahab returned home, he told Jezebel everything Elijah had done and she, in anger, threatened Elijah with death. When he heard about her threats, he crumbled in fear and went into a state of depression. Jezebel does not go away easily. (1 Kings 18 – 19:1)

"And Ahab told Jezebel all that Elijah had done, also how he had executed all the prophets with the sword. Then Jezebel sent a messenger to Elijah, saying, 'So let the gods do to me, and more also, if I do not make your life as the life of one of them by tomorrow about this time.' And when he saw that, he arose and ran for his life, and went to Beersheba, which belongs to Judah, and left his servant there." (1 Kings 19:1-3

NKJV)

Jezebel decided she was going to kill the man of God. What happened to this powerful prophet? Instead of standing up to Jezebel, and fighting her, he fled to the hills, wishing he could die. Elijah became depressed over this confrontation and actually begged God to kill him. Though she didn't lay a hand on him, Jezebel's words did more damage than if she had struck him with a sword.

"But he himself went a day's journey into the wilderness, and came and sat down under a broom tree. And he prayed that he might die, and said, "It is enough! Now, Lord, take my life, for I am no better than my fathers!" (1 Kings 19:4 NKJV)

Imagine how many leaders have been driven to the cave of depression and apathy: driven to the mindset of, "Why bother? Why try anymore? Or, God, come and take me now." The Jezebel spirit isolates in order to eradicate. If this spirit was able to do this to Elijah, it is quite capable of doing the same thing to others, including ourselves. It is time to come out of the cave of depression. In this cave, tunnel vision causes you to lose perspective preventing you from seeing the bigger picture. Therefore, God called Elijah out of the cave so he could see that his ministry was not over; he was about to become greater and stronger. The Lord instructed him to anoint Hazael as king over Syria, Jehu as king over Israel, and Elisha as the prophet who would take his place. These men were assigned to judge those who were in disobedience to God's laws.

"Then the Lord said to him: "Go, return on your way to the Wilderness of Damascus; and when you arrive,

anoint Hazael as king over Syria. Also, you shall anoint Jehu the son of Nimshi as king over Israel. And Elisha the son of Shaphat of Abel Meholah you shall anoint as prophet in your place. It shall be that whoever escapes the sword of Hazael, Jehu will kill; and whoever escapes the sword of Jehu, Elisha will kill." (1 Kings 19:15-17 NKJV)

Those who escaped King Hazael's sword, King Jehu would kill; and those who escaped King Jehu's sword, Elisha would kill. God permitted no man to do them wrong, for He commanded they not be touched nor harmed. God has a hatred for people who cause the man, or woman, of God undue stress which could send them into the cave of despair and depression. Like Elijah, this can cause God's people to question their calling.

"When they went from one nation to another, And, from one kingdom to another people, He permitted no man to do them wrong; Yes, He rebuked kings for their sakes, Saying, "Do not touch My anointed ones, And, do My prophets no harm." (1 Chronicles 16:20-22 NKJV)

Just as God dealt with Korah in the book of Numbers, He will also deal with those who cause division in His church and within His leadership. (Numbers 16:31) As a result of Korah rebelling against Moses, God caused the earth to open up and swallow him, his family, as well as all those who followed him in his rebellion. Today, God will turn those who cause divisions, and offenses, within the church, over to themselves which opens them up for attack. They will destroy themselves from within.

"Now I urge you, brethren, note those who cause divisions and offenses, contrary to the doctrine which you learned, and avoid them. For those who are such do not serve our Lord Jesus Christ, but their own belly, and by smooth words and flattering speech deceive the hearts of the simple. For your obedience has become known to all. Therefore, I am glad on your behalf; but I want you to be wise in what is good, and simple concerning evil. And the God of peace will crush Satan under your feet shortly..." (Romans 16:17-20 NKJV)

JEHU'S REACTION

The first thing Jehu did was ride, with his army, straight to Jezebel's castle. He was not going there to make a treaty; he went there to kill her and to destroy this wicked and perverse spirit.

"Now when Jehu had come to Jezreel, Jezebel heard of it; and she put paint on her eyes and adorned her head and looked through a window." (2 Kings 9:30)

As Jezebel saw the horsemen's clouds rising over the horizon, she proceeded to dress, and prepare, herself in order to seduce King Jehu. God had rejected King Ahab and Jezebel knew it. Therefore, because this spirit is never loyal, she immediately released Ahab and set the stage to seduce another. This is exactly what happens within the church. This spirit will move from leader to leader and from church to church in its goal of controlling people through seduction.

When Jehu saw Jezebel, she was hanging out her window anticipating how he would fall for her immodest pose. She, smugly, expected to catch Jehu in her web of seduction and deceit. However, the King had another agenda and it did not include being seduced. He rode in under the banner of Elijah, the prophet, with a command, from God, to kill her; he would strike her down and destroy this controlling spirit.

*"Then, as Jehu entered at the gate, she said, "Is it peace Zimri, murderer of your master?" 32) And he looked up at the window, and said, **"Who is on my side?** Who?*

The first thing Jezebel did was to question Jehu's motive for being at her castle. However, he didn't answer her, but asked, "Who is on my side?" He wanted to know if there was anyone, in the castle, who had not been bewitched by Jezebel. He also didn't enter her domain for risk of being influenced by her unholy, beguiling nature. It is important to understand, it is impossible to sit down and negotiate with this spirit; don't even try, she will not change. And, her instigated problems cannot be addressed, nor dealt with, by those who have fallen for her seductive ways. It must be resolved by those who are able to expose and drive out this enemy.

*"...So, two or three eunuchs looked out at him. Then he said, "**Throw her down.**" So, they threw her down, and some of her blood spattered on the wall and on the horses; and he trampled her underfoot. And when he had gone in, he ate and drank..."* (2 Kings 9:32-34 NKJV)

After discovering there were several eunuchs on his side, Jehu commanded Jezebel to be thrown to the ground. Jehu challenged them in order to prove whose side they were on so they threw her out the window.

Eunuchs are palace officials who have been castrated to prevent them from being seduced by the queen. They are generally assigned to her chambers due to their castration preventing them from having sexual relations.

In the body of Christ, spiritual eunuchs are those who have dedicated themselves to the Lord's work, as well as, the protection of leadership. Spiritual eunuchs are those whose ears have been circumcised, ***"Faith cometh by hearing, and hearing by the word of God."*** (Romans 10:17) Their lives have been altered in such a way as to protect them from being seduced by the Jezebel spirit. They are the ones who expose, destroy, and rid the church of its presence.

The church is in need spiritual eunuchs; they should stand up and be counted. Can you be altered for Christ? It is in the altering that Jezebel's words lose their power to beguile, or trick, people against the church, or against His anointed ones.

*"Now I beseech you, brethren, **mark them** which cause divisions and offences contrary to the doctrine which ye have learned; and avoid them. For they that are such serve not our Lord Jesus Christ, but their own belly; and by good words and fair speeches deceive the hearts of the simple."* (Romans 16:17-18 KJV)

*"Brethren, be followers together of me, and **mark them** which walk so as ye have us for an example. (For many walk, of whom I have told you often, and now tell you even weeping, that they are the enemies of the cross of Christ: Whose end is destruction, whose God is their belly, and whose glory is in their shame, who mind earthly things.)"* (Philippians 3:17-19 KJV)

People with hidden agendas don't come to our churches in order to promote the gospel; they are not about Jesus. Their purpose is to cause division and strife within the body of Christ.

The Bible clearly tells us to, "**mark them.**" In Greek, the word "**mark**" means to take aim, to box them in as one who is taking aim to shoot. It can be assumed, for the church, it means to take a picture of those operating under the Jezebel spirit and show their faces to everyone. Why? so they can be avoided. It is important for church folk to stay away from these people. Unfortunately, they can do an abundance of harm to an individual's mind. So, run from them; for, a good run will always be better than a bad stand.

This type of insurrectionist is too smooth to out talk; she will, eventually, be able to persuade others to her way of thinking. This spirit, more commonly, operates in women, however, it does not mean a man cannot walk in this spirit as well.

BREAK COVENANT WITH THESE PEOPLE

Maintaining fellowship with a controlling and disloyal spirit can cause a person to fall under the same curse as the insurrectionist. This spirit has the power to mask, and deceive, while taking on many different looks and forms. Breaking covenant may not be something wanted, but the desire to hold on can be deceptive.

DECEPTIONS TO LOOK FOR

- *I can handle it.* Even Superman had his kryptonite. Proverbs 31:30 states that charm is powerful and deceptive.
- *I am special to them.* They prey upon our

insecurities along with our need for acceptance. 2 Samuel 15:5 states, *"And so it was, whenever anyone came near to bow down to him, that he would put out his hand and take him and kiss him."*

- **They are my friends.** You may think your friendship with an insurrectionist will not affect your connection to the local church, but it will. If you lay with dogs, you will get fleas!
- **They love God so, why should we judge them?** If they really loved God, they would not alter God's way of doing things, nor would they flatter and manipulate people in the way they do. They love themselves, not the things of God.
- **I can help them.** Those operating according to this spirit think they are helping you. So, what makes you think you can help them? To help them is to correct them, however, an insurrectionist hates to be corrected. Instead of admitting he is wrong, he will cut off the relationship with you first.

    o Many of us have had the false notion we can restore insurrectionists back to the kingdom; the enemy thrives on this type of sentiment. It gives him greater inroads of influence for the purpose of taking advantage of, and shipwrecking, your faith. His main goal is to advance his agenda. ***"Reject a divisive man after the first and second admonition."*** (Titus 3:10 NKJV)

NOTE: Deception means not knowing you are being deceived. Many people think they have more discernment than they actually do and they also forget they are dealing with a demonic spirit. And, the purpose of a controlling personality is to come against God's established authority. They seek to divide His kingdom.

David believed he could restore Absalom back to the kingdom. However, David's love was not enough and he could not help him. Instead, David made the decision to give mercy where God had already established His law; *Never rewrite your theology to accommodate your tragedies.* This will only cause more crises.

REACTIONS THAT CREATED DAVID'S CRISIS

- His feelings outweighed God's laws.
- He felt he had to prove his compassion to others; putting his kingdom above God's laws.
- Because of the sin in David's own life, he overlooked his son's, therefore, tolerating his enemy by not confronting it.
- Rejection outweighed the law of reasoning.
- His failure as a father impaired his ability in certain aspects of his Kingship.
- David's fear of rejection caused him to love the wrong people. He loved those that hated him and hated those that loved him.
- His lust outweighed loyalty to his assignment.

> "Envy is the pain and distress you feel over someone else's success!"

ROOT ALWAYS PRODUCES FRUIT

I believe envy is the number one root that produces the fruit of disloyalty! Envy begins when I am not content with what I have or with what I am doing; it is an inner feeling of not measuring up. It is a feeling of discontentment with regard to another's advantages, success, and possessions. You can be assured, coveting another's success breeds discontentment.

FACTS ABOUT ENVY

- Envy is not grateful for what it has.
- Does not celebrate the success of others.
- Is never secure in itself.
- Cannot stop comparing itself to others.
- Is competitive.
- Will never be content due to its internal struggles.
- Stops the flow of worship.
- Causes bitterness and unforgiveness.
- Is evil.

*"Now the works of the flesh are evident, which are: adultery, fornication, uncleanness, lewdness, idolatry, sorcery, hatred, contentions, jealousies, outbursts of wrath, selfish ambitions, dissensions, heresies, **envy**, murders, drunkenness, revelries, and the like; of which I tell you beforehand, just as I also told you in time past, that those who practice such things will not inherit the kingdom of God."* (Galatians 5:19-21 NKJV)

Envy is empowered by imbedded bitterness. Bitterness is a feeling of antagonism, hostility, or resentfulness. It can flare up when people see that God has blessed someone else with whatever they were wanting themselves. One of Absalom's greatest sins was envy; it also caused Esau to become bitter over

Jacob.

Envy is developed by a self-seeking mind-set. Self-seekers always create strife and division. Strife means vigorous or bitter conflict, discord, or antagonism. Some call it self-ambition. Envy is fueled, and maintained, by a self-seeking, self-ambitious person.

Envy speaks the loudest, is boastful, and is rooted in the kind of pride that produces a boastful, bragging attitude. Envy is revealed when a person consistently talks about their own accomplishments rather than listening to someone else's. Unfortunately, when envy is present, strife usually occurs.

"For where envy and self-seeking exist, confusion and every evil thing are there." (James 3:16 NKJV)

The answer for overcoming, the spirit of envy, is found in James 4:1-3: *"Where do wars and fights come from among you? Do they not come from your desires for pleasure that war in your members? You lust and do not have. You murder and covet and cannot obtain. You fight and war. Yet, you do not have because you do not ask. You ask and do not receive, because you ask amiss, that you may spend it on your pleasures."*

SEVEN WEAPONS TO STOP ENVY

- **A PURE MIND:** A mind free from defilement.
- **A PEACEABLE MIND:** A mind free from contention and debate.
- **A GENTLE MIND:** A mind that is kind, courteous, and considerate of others.
- **A TEACHABLE MIND:** A mind that is willing to

listen, change, and grow. The opposite of being stubborn.
- **A MERCIFUL MIND:** A mind that is free from judging others and is full of grace. Mercy is a seed.
- **AN IMPARTIAL MIND:** A mind free from prejudices; one that is impartial and does not play favorites.
- **A TRANSPARENT MIND:** A mind free of masks; they are transparent. They don't have anything to hide.

CHAPTER FOUR

THE PORTRAIT OF THE SPIRIT OF CONTROL

When I was younger, my life was filled with fear. So, I know firsthand what it is like to be under a spirit of control. I was afraid of the bullies who would walk the hallways, of my school, and pick on the guys who were small or who were different; they would pick on the ones who would not fight back. Even though I tried, I was afraid of failing. And, I was afraid of not being loved or not being good enough.

All these fears, along with being molested as a child, caused me to have some deep, serious wounds which caused me to second-guess myself. I became a breeding ground that enabled the spirit of control to sow its seeds of control into my life. However, thank God, I have been healed of those wounds and am confident to take on the challenges in front of me. When I decided to come clean with God, and myself, the healing process began. Then, healing came after many years of mentorship, facing reality, and avoiding the shadow of lies.

EIGHT SIGNS OF THE SPIRIT OF CONTROL

- *They focus on themselves rather than people.* They have an all-about-me attitude where ego plays a big part in stimulating their mind.

- *They continually remind people of their authority. An authority which isn't based on genuine, Godly character, their message or their lifestyle.* The core trait of the Jezebel spirit is **false authority.**

- *To the spirit of control, if you mention a*

problem, then you become the problem. When a person exposes a problem, then, the controlling spirit will accuse them of causing the problem. They do this in order to mask and hide their own weaknesses; they like pointing fingers at others.

- *They constantly take loyalty tests.* Loyalty is demanded by the spirit of control; Not loyalty to Christ but to the spirit of control. Often, if you leave or do not follow their agenda, repercussions will be threatened.

- *Their weapons are secrecy, surprises, and suspense in order to create chaos and confusion.* They are "**the only ones who know**"; the only ones who have access to truth. They will hide what is inappropriate, and only reveal what is appropriate. The Jezebel spirit will go to great lengths to avoid being honest, open, and *transparent.* Though it is a lie, she will state those characteristics as being the virtues she possesses.

- *They teach unbalanced doctrines including: prophecy, biblical law, esoteric methods of biblical interpretation, and spiritual methods. They do this without presenting the whole counsel of God.* There cannot be a biblically balanced presentation of the word of God when there is a Jezebel spirit in control of a group. Being biblically balanced would defeat their efforts at manipulating, and intimidating, people through the twisting of the scriptures.

- ***They will run from, and fight, any source of correction.*** They will do whatever is necessary to force their lie, as truth, upon the people. When confronted, they act as though you have attacked them as well as questioned their loyalty. Watch out! In the next season, this person will attempt to destroy you.

- ***They insist on being promoted, then, question why you have not discerned their anointing for leadership.*** They act as though the organization is their focus. In reality, they are building connections with those you have spent time building up and training.

TECHNIQUES USED IN CONTROL

- EXCESS FLATTER. People want to believe they are special and will readily accept being part of a "special" group considered as "insiders." Because most people want to be part of an "elite" group, the Jezebel spirit is more than willing to accommodate that desire. And, when it best serves its purpose, the Jezebel spirit will appear to be a loving and gracious person who oozes and drips with flattery.

- PROMISES TO GIVE POSITIONS OF AUTHORITY. The flattery continues by urging people to use their "unique, personal talents" to guide and teach others. The Jezebel spirit is skilled at prophesying great things which most people believe is the Holy Spirit endorsing repressed, or hidden, personal desires to be in charge. This is a type of false prophecy that can be heady, exhilarating, influential, and motivating.

- **A POSITION OF GREAT AUTHORITY IS ASSUMED.** They will contact you again, and again, to attempt to get you to attend meetings, parties, or other special events. They will use other socially, manipulative tactics, in an effort, to recruit you into their group—all for your own good, of course. The Jezebel spirit will, quickly, lose its sphere of influence if it doesn't continue to add members to its cult.

- **YOU WILL BE ASKED TO RESPOND TO QUESTIONS WITH ANSWERS THAT CONFIRM THEIR AUTHORITY.** This can be in the form of group psychology. Through questions derived from a hidden agenda, the Jezebel spirit continues to flatter while making it appear as though the answers given are by the person's own free will. However, the questions were formed in order for the answers to reflect support of the Jezebel point of view. This is a manipulative ploy enabling the Jezebel spirit to retain its false authority. This spirit will plant false ideas of greatness, in an attempt, to assert its authority in what it considers to be clever, non-intrusive, and subtle techniques. **THE FORMER FLATTERY IT EXTENDED WILL NOW BE USED AGAINST YOU.** The former wild praise, then the loss of esteem, causes the resulting disappointment to serve as a powerful force motivating dissenters to "get with the program." In so many words, they will inform you that you "owe" them for your blessings. The Jezebel spirit does not like to disappoint those who, initially, claim to be impressed with them. This is especially true when a controlling person has assumed a position of authority, over an individual, claiming to have "selected" that person for membership in a special group. This person will also use disappointment as a weapon leading you to believe that you have disappointed God. It will focus on your failures, including, when it comes to conducting yourself as an up-and-coming, powerful religious leader.

- **EARLY ON, THE RULES OF THE GAME WILL CHANGE. WITH NO WARNING, THE GAME WILL PROCEED AS THOUGH NOTHING UNUSUAL HAPPENED.** Such, "bait and switch," tactics are typical of those who, attempt to, recruit others into positions of authority. At this stage, most people slowly internalize the Jezebel point of view and repress any doubts they may have had. They now believe the Jezebel point of view is their own; the fundamental components of their own thought processes. The Jezebel spirit knows the power of the human ego. It will feed a man's ego what is necessary in order for him to become self-centered as well as focused on the "spiritual authority" he deems God wants him to have. This is like building castles in the sand.

- **THE JEZEBEL SPIRIT WILL CONTRADICT ITSELF THROUGHOUT THE COURSE OF ANY RELATIONSHIP.** They will cover their tracks by, repeatedly, verbalizing the objections used to manipulate you from the start. They believe the view people have, of themselves, would make it difficult for them to fully recognize the extent in which they have been controlled. Jezebels are very clever in making people believe they are in

control of their own lives. However, this places them in the worst kind of bondage; one human to another. They can be very convincing when they want you to believe that you also have spiritual authority which is, in itself, false.
- **THE DESIRE TO AVOID FEELINGS OF DISILLUSIONMENT AND ISOLATION.** This could be a powerful factor motivating people to remain connected to a manipulator. Even after joining the special group and, though, their extraordinary hopes, and desires, are dashed, they still choose to be connected. The need for relationship and significance can be the coveted prize in any group of people. The spirit of control is familiar with the desire to preserve one's own *illusions in the fulfillment of its hopes and desires; it expects that all Jezebel's tactics will override any logical analysis. Though logic* can motivate, the controlling spirit knows **emotions are much more powerful and will override logic.** Jezebels also know enthusiasm can reinforce a person's emotions beyond anything else that can be done.

THE CONTROLLING SPIRIT

There is a distinction between the **spirit of control** and fulfilling one's responsibilities with diligence. True leaders can have the tendency to micromanage which gives the appearance of control, however, this is not a spirit. Many people

> "Discernment Is When the Spirit Is Telling You Something That Your Mind Isn't."

confuse the two, then rationalize their controlling spirit by saying, "W*ell, I'm just trying to live up to my* *responsibilities."* It is vital for every person to understand the difference, then, discern between a spirit of control and leadership gifting.

To live up to responsibilities means being diligent to work hard in order to fulfill every responsibility within the home, family-life, work, and relationships. And, Ecclesiastes 9:10 commands, "Whatever your hand finds to do, do it with your might." It is not this way with a controlling spirit. They work hard at manipulating individuals, events, and circumstances in order to make every situation turn to their advantage. Controlling people get very upset when things do not go their way. It doesn't matter if they are in their home, at work, or any other place, they are convinced that the world will fall apart if they are not in control. For this person to be comfortable, control is a must.

Someone who has to be in control thinks nothing can be done right. They believe nothing good can happen without their input and direction; some even think God can't do anything without their help. There are people who think they know better than God, that He needs their input, ideas, and plans in order for everything to move in the right direction. They believe their way is the only right, proper, and beneficial way. Of course, because they believe they are the center of the universe, controlling people have only their own best interests in mind.

The controlling spirit is the number one enemy of faith. A controlling spirit is one of the biggest hindrances to an individual's faith; it leaves little room for trust, in God, to operate. When exercising their dominance over others, a controlling person will give no leeway for individuality, or freedom. They end up ruining relationships, causing isolation and loneliness, and ultimately squeezing all faith, with God, out of the lives of those who have fallen prey to their tactics; the Holy Spirit is very grieved over this.

Because the Holy Spirit is a gentleman, He cannot work in the life of someone harboring control issues. The Holy Spirit is completely blocked from operating in the life of an individual with a controlling spirit. Because of this, they are not able to come to the knowledge of the truth making faith, in Christ, nearly impossible. As a result, their only alternative is trusting in themselves until they are delivered from this demonic stronghold.

A controlling person worships self. In this individual, self sits on the throne of their heart and rules everything. The only perspective they are able to see, and understand, is their own. If another person's thoughts, or ideas, are contrary to their own, they are deemed unacceptable. And, if pushed, they will fight, "tooth and nail," to defeat that person.

People with a controlling spirit are...
- Heady and intoxicating
- High-minded
- Head-strong
- Overbearing
- Merciless
- Highly opinionated
- Selfish
- Uncaring people who fight, against all odds, to have things their way.

2 Kings 4 gives an example of the danger of a controlling spirit. Also, how to be delivered from it.

"Elisha went back to Gilgal. At the time, there was a famine in the land. The guild prophets were sitting

before him, and he said to his servant, 'Put the big pot on the fire, and boil some soup for the prophets.' 39) One of them went out to the field to gather vegetables and came upon a wild vine, from which he filled the front of his cloak with wild squash. 40) Then they poured it out for the men to eat; but on tasting it, they cried, 'Man of God! There's death in that pot!' And they couldn't eat it. 41) But he said, 'Bring some flour.' He threw it in the pot, then said, 'Pour it out for the people to eat.' This time there was nothing harmful in the pot." (2 Kings 4:38-41 Complete Jewish Study Bible)

This scripture reveals how the controlling nature fashions its intrusion into God's provision. This event could have brought misery and, possible, death to the whole community. An individual like this will always seek to improve upon God's plan and purpose, usually with devastating results. They hurt the people who have yielded to their evil schemes; including their families, their communities, along with the people of God. They also hurt the work of God.

This passage shows there was a famine in the land. And, because most people have never lived through a famine, they do not understand the effects it can have on the population. Only those who visit other countries experiencing famine, or who watch documentaries revealing the devastation famines cause, have a glimpse of the destruction and death they can bring. In times of stress, such as a famine, be very intentional. Stress can be an opportunity to trust God or, it can become a window for disaster. It

> **"God was, and is, and always will be in the miracle working business."**

can be a time for looking to God's faithfulness or, it can become a doorway to calamity.

At this time, the seminary, or school of the prophets gave Elisha the title of, "President"; he was responsible for the training and well-being of the prophets who were, obviously, affected by the famine. After returning from his preaching mission, Elisha checked on the community, of believers, within his charge and realized, as a result of the famine, they were hungry. Then, he instructed his servant to get a large pot and make a stew big enough to feed everyone. Though, the question was, "how, due to the famine, would the servant accomplish this?" Where would he get the necessary items for the stew? Fortunately, in tough seasons, God always provided for His faithful servants. He is able to bring refreshing in times of disaster and He proves His sufficiency during times of need. He honors those who honor Him; He is light in the midst of darkness; He can bring water out of a rock; and, He can multiply the little so there will be more than enough. God supernaturally provided stew through the faith of the prophet, Elisha.

God was, and is, and always will be in the miracle working business. God is a miracle working God and, that will never change. He is supernatural in the midst of calamity, natural disaster, judgment, and stressful times. God will, always, move on behalf of His faithful children.

In Genesis, in the land of Canaan, there was a devastating famine that threatened to bring about the destruction of Jacob and his children. This meant the whole nation of Israel, including the lineage from which the Messiah would come, could be wiped out. However, in order to spare them, God sent Joseph, ahead of the famine, to the land of Egypt. *God is always strategic in His planning.* Then, in Exodus, while Egypt was plunged into darkness, God supernaturally provided light for His children. Also, in 1 Kings, He supernaturally provided for Elijah, the prophet, during the famine that struck the land of Israel.

"For the LORD God is a sun and shield: the LORD will give grace and glory: no good thing will he withhold from them that walk uprightly." (Psalms 84:11 KJV)

He did not say perfect but, "upright." In Hebrew, this means to *be undefiled, without spot, sound, complete, and whole*. Being washed in the blood of Jesus, and being under the grace of God, enables this to happen. And, to be upright, has to do with one's attitude, motivation, and condition of the heart. God does not expect absolute, sinless, perfection. He knows that will only happen when people are face to face with the risen Lord; and, when they have the same resurrected body as Jesus. However, He does expect His people to walk blameless before Him.

Being blameless is different than being perfect. Walking blameless is understanding when, and how, to repent. It means being so sensitive to God we, immediately, fall under conviction when sin takes place. Or, we recognize the moment we begin going in the wrong direction. At the leading of His Spirit, we do not wait, delay, or resist changing direction; and, we quickly repent in order to keep fellowship, with God, open and alive.

Today, in the church, too many people hide behind semantics saying; **"Well, I confessed my sins a long time ago."** *Really! But, are you living a consistently repentant, or changed, lifestyle?* Biblical repentance means to turn around and go a different direction. However, instead of altering our lifestyles, the power of salvation and eternal life have been watered down and, as a result, we tend to stay the same. Because our salvation was paid for by Jesus' death on the cross, God expects us to turn, or repent, from our wicked ways.

Westernized Christianity and post-modern culture have created gods that fit neatly into people's lifestyles. Instead of allowing our flesh to be crucified with Christ, we have fashioned gods after our own likes and dislikes; they become our servants rather than, us, serving the Father's desires. These gods will not judge our actions but, will love us, no matter what we do. In our minds, we can take them, or leave them. And, we believe, without us, they are helpless. We have created gods who will tickle our ears rather than tell us the truth. **This makes for an atmosphere that feeds a controlling spirit.**

Among God's people, one of the greatest tragedies in today's world is refusing to believe that God is supernatural; that He is out of the supernatural business. Most church goers fail to believe that Jesus is Lord and that He is sitting upon the throne of the universe. Instead, God has been brought down to man's image of Him. And, rather than honoring, serving, worshiping, and pleasing Him, they serve the image of their own making. They serve an image of "self." Unfortunately, most people who do this, don't realize they are deceived. This is why Jeremiah 17:9 states, *"The heart is deceitful above all things, and desperately wicked: who can know it?"*

So, in the midst of the famine, and through the faith of Elisha, God supernaturally provided for the guild prophets. Elisha requested his servant get a big pot, then, make a stew for the people. After doing so, it was discovered that, due to the squash from the wild vine, the stew was not fit to eat. We don't know who collected the vegetables, cut them up, then put them in the stew, however, we are told, "they didn't know what they were." A controlling spirit always looks to improve God's recipe by adding unknown ingredients to the mix. It would also seem, the servant wanted to take credit for feeding the prophets. His attitude could have been, "Well, I know God provides, but not without my help."

"One of them went out to the field to gather vegetables and came upon a wild vine, from which he filled the front of his cloak with wild squash. On returning he cut them up and put them into the stew; they didn't know what they were." (II Kings 4:39)

If you don't see the humor in this, then you have not dealt with a controlling spirit. If you find yourself grimacing and gritting your teeth then, maybe, you need to be delivered from the spirit of control. Faith will not work as long as this spirit is in charge. Some people believe they need to help God in order for the job to get done. They are impatient and will not wait to receive God's provision. Instead of being the servant, or the child of God at the table, they want to be the master; the one calling the shots. They want to improve upon God's recipe.

It is not wise to think you can improve upon God's provision. Without knowing, this man added death to the stew God had provided. What would have been deemed a miracle of provision, was now neutralized and, became a disaster. It is important to understand, God wants to work in,

> "Never Try to Improve on God's Recipe for Change."

and through, every person; for every individual to meet the conditions of His promises. And, because He will do what He has said, He expects people to trust Him with all their hearts.

Cain did not like the idea of offering animal sacrifices, the shedding of their blood, as God had taught Adam and Eve. Instead, he decided to approach God on his own terms. As a result, God rejected his offerings, and he became filled with anger and jealousy. However, Abel, his brother, did as instructed and his sacrifice was accepted. Because of this, Cain killed Abel. He would not admit that his own failure, in following God's instructions, was the cause of His rejection. Cain **had poisoned the pot;** he had poisoned his heart, then caused physical death to his brother. Ultimately, he brought spiritual death to himself.

There are many examples of this is the Bible: 1) the sons of Aaron, Moses' brother, wanted to worship God in their own way. **They poisoned the pot.** 2) The sons of Eli, the priest, decided to worship God in their own way and brought defeat to the nation of Israel. Ultimately, it ended in their own destruction. **They poisoned the pot.** 3) Without Samuel, the prophet, King Saul sacrificed to God. He was out of the will of God and brought disaster to the nation of Israel. **He poisoned the pot.** And, 4) In Acts, Ananias and Sapphira lied to the Holy Spirit and brought death upon themselves. **They poisoned the pot.**

When people do things their own way, rather than God's, they poison the pot. The blessings of God are hindered and are stopped, dead in their tracks as a result. As a Christ follower, it is dangerous to operate your business, run your ministry, raise your children, or serve God in any way contrary to His way. By doing this, you will poison the pot and end up with devastating consequences.

Fortunately, our story, in 1 Kings 4, ends on a good note. Elisha states, in verse 41, *"But he said, 'Bring some flour.' He threw it in the pot, then said, 'Pour it out for the people to eat.' This time there was nothing harmful in the pot."* Because the flour was put in the pot, the poison was neutralized. In the scriptures, flour is a type of the resurrected Christ. It is the product of the crushing and milling of the grain of wheat. And in John, chapter 12, Jesus said, *"unless a grain of wheat falls to the ground and dies, it cannot produce a harvest."* Here, He was speaking of Himself. Jesus was the flour thrown into the pot of death; He brings death back to life again. His life neutralizes our death sentence due to the sin produced on the wild vine of the advocate. Since Jesus was crushed, He put an end to man's efforts of obtaining eternal life without Him.

- Jesus is the flour that ended ceremonial law.
- Jesus is the flour that raised us from death.
- Jesus is the flour that saves us from ourselves.
- Jesus is the flour that prevents the disaster caused by a controlling spirit.

Only Jesus Christ, the resurrected One, can nullify the power of the controlling spirit; this enables you to complete His work. The question is, will you allow Jesus to do this? Will you allow His flour to come into the pot, of your life, in order to neutralize the poison of the controlling spirit? If not, it will stop the miracle of His blessing and provision. If deliverance is needed from this spirit, ask God! Do this so you can be free to serve Him; free to do His will rather than your own.

CHAPTER FIVE

Loyalty Is a Rare Gift

*"...And give my son Solomon a **loyal heart** to keep Your commandments and Your testimonies and Your statutes, to do all these things, and to build the temple for which I have made provision."* (1 Chronicles 29:19 NKJV)

In this scripture, David is praying for the next King of Israel; Solomon, his son. He asked, the Lord, for Solomon to have a loyal heart in order to keep God's commandments, testimonies, statutes, and many other things. Just as it was important for the King of Israel, it is necessary for every congregant, in partnership with the church's leadership, to walk in loyalty. The dictionary defines loyalty as, "Faithful to the constituted authority of one's country. Faithful to those persons, ideals, etc. that one is under obligation to defend, support, or be true to, relating to, or indicating loyalty." Loyalty demands following through with commitments even when circumstances change. Unfortunately, this is the greatest thing missing from today's pulpit and pew.

Disloyalty is easy to see due to the vast number of people who walk away from their churches. After desiring to be connected, within a year, they leave. For whatever reason, they begin to cool off, then they show signs of disinterest in the church as well as its functions. Their attendance starts to waver and their attitude changes. Suddenly, they begin complaining about the pastor, leaders, and congregants they do not like. Though they were once loyal, fired up members, they are now angry and bitter. Disloyalty is a cancer that must be destroyed so that the Kingdom of God can continue to expand.

As I was sitting with some great men of God,

one began discussing how a loyal member of his congregation, suddenly, rose up against him. This prompted another to comment, "I tell you what; **loyalty is a rare gift to have.**" Through experience, I believe this to be true.

Loyalty is measured through time. Many church members appear to be loyal, however, loyalty is measured through time. Loyalty is remaining, or sticking, with the church even when things get rough. To understand this better, read my book, "*God's Unwavering Faithfulness.*" Here, I touched on the difference between a **servant worker and a servant attitude**. The heart of a servant is much different than that of a person who does a servant's work. Many times, people begin serving their leaders based on an agenda, rather than, from a heart desiring to serve. It is not possible to, truly, serve and stay loyal as long as there is an ulterior motive at play. Eventually, when their purpose has been achieved, the servant worker will rise up against the one whom they have been "serving." Unfortunately, he is not interested in what God has taught the Pastor, nor does he care about him. However, he is interested in what the Pastor has; **THE SERVANT WORKER WANTS YOUR STUFF!**

How do I know when someone is a servant? **When I treat you as a servant and you don't become angry or agitated.** It is important to refrain from allowing people to become servants until they have passed the test of time. Time will prove their loyalty, reveal their motives, and expose their hidden agendas. And, as these disloyal attributes are uncovered, it is vital to, immediately, separate yourself from that person's influence. Otherwise, they could be

> "The Proof of Loyalty is measured through time."

the one deciding whether your next season will be good or bad. In connecting with them, you are connecting with their disobedient lifestyle as well as anything left undone in their last season; you will also share in their consequences.

Jonah ran from God's instructions by jumping on a ship headed away from Nineveh; away from the presence of the Lord. As a result of his disobedience, everyone on the ship experienced trouble. As they were on their way to Tarshish, a great storm developed causing danger to the ship. Fearful of sinking, the men began hurling the cargo into the sea in order to lighten the ship's load. They believed this catastrophe was, somehow, their fault and began calling on their gods to see who they could blame. Instead of helping with the cargo, Jonah lay sleeping in the stern of the ship. So, the men decided to cast lots and discovered it was Jonah who caused God to unleash this terrible storm. Therefore, Jonah instructed the men to throw him overboard and the storm would cease.

It is possible, many of us could be living through storms that were not scheduled, but came about as a result of wrong people in our lives. Unfortunately, currently, we could be experiencing problems that were not meant for us.

QUALIFY THE PEOPLE YOU DESIRE TO BE CONNECTED WITH

Loyalty is a decision of the will, not an emotional response of the heart. Loyalty is not an emotion, or a feeling, but a decision. If loyalty were, simply, based on feelings, then Jesus Himself may have become disloyal. And, I can tell you, there will be times, while serving the leader, when feelings and emotions will be strained beyond their limit. The moment people give voice to emotions, the enemy will begin to deceive. Emotions will declare, *"You're not appreciated, no one ever notices your effort nor your willingness to serve."* A, "what about me," attitude will state, "*no one cares... no one loves me... no one notices me.*"

If you haven't made the commitment to follow or the decision to be loyal; or, if you haven't made the decision to remain, to stay faithful, and to abide, you will most assuredly make the wrong decisions. Then, chances are, you will leave the place God would bless you beyond measure. This has happened in my ministry. Some people needed to leave, however, others left due to hurt feelings or misunderstandings. Unfortunately, because of this, they left with wrong attitudes, rather than being sent, by God, to their next place. Because they "went," they usually find themselves living in a nomadic state instead of doing great things for God. They find themselves wandering from place to place never seeming to fit anywhere. As a result of leaving the ministry in the wrong way, they fail to develop the correct mind-set for being "sent" into their next season. Don't be fooled, churches are full of such nomadic people. Nomads, or wanderers, will always be disloyal.

Some time ago, a family, who was wounded and hurting, began attending The Favor Life Church. Their marriage was on the brink of divorce; and, their children were angry and bitter over what was happening in their home. I made the mistake of not qualifying their purpose of being at The Favor Life Church nor of what had taken place at their previous church. I spent time counseling them and praying for them. But, as soon as their marriage began to heal, they did a one-hundred eighty-degree

> **"Trust but Verify!"**

turn. In the beginning, their leadership skills seemed valuable enough to be a help to the ministry. However, what a deception! They had, what I call, "the *entry of the palace but content of a hut.*" To make a long story short, they left The Favor Life Church and moved to another. Sometime later, I discovered they left their previous church after becoming angry with the senior pastor. Not only did they leave, but they caused a church split. Then, they tried, but failed, to start another church; their marriage suffered as a result. It was, at this point, they entered my ship (The Favor Life Church) as a Jonah. Now, I encourage every Pastor to qualify their people, qualify everyone. "Trust, but verify" will be my motto from now on.

I should have asked revealing questions but the church has been conditioned to receive everybody. Sadly, this enables the Jezebel spirit to enter our churches with the potential to destroy what has been built. To prevent this from happening, leaders should always qualify those who proclaim leadership skills. The purpose of the Pastor, or Shepherd, is to lead their sheep to green pastures, anoint their heads with oil, watch for wolves, etc. In order to protect the whole sheep herd, a Pastor should, immediately, kill the influence of a wolf whenever it is revealed. Wolves in sheep's clothing can only be discovered as the Pastor's become, proper, sheep inspectors.

Loyalty is remaining in submission even after agreement ends. The truest test of loyalty is when a person can stay connected to leadership even when they fail to agree with the decisions being made. By sticking with them during seasons of confusion, the church will grow and become healthier. Loyalty allows time for the leader to build upon his plans.

Loyalty is when a person lines up, in agreement, to the vision. When relating to marriage, people like to use the word submission. However, the truth is, no husband really wants a submissive wife; he wants a wife who walks in agreement. The same is true in ministry. Ministers of God become frustrated when their people only walk in submission. When this happens, the vision, of the church, becomes clouded and they will need constant persuading of its purpose. However, those who are in agreement help take the struggle out of success.

> "Lack of loyalty is one of the major causes of failure in every walk of life."
> Napoleon Hill

"Behold, how good and how pleasant it is for brethren to dwell together in unity! It is like the precious oil upon the head, running down on the beard, the beard of Aaron, Running down on the edge of his garments." (Psalm 133:1-2 NKJV)

Agreement compares to the oil.

Love doesn't, necessarily, mean you will be loyal. God, as Love, is always loyal; however, human love can be severely lacking in this regard. God was faithful to humankind even while they were sinners; but, the weakness of human love causes man to abort all commitment and loyalty when those feelings fade. Because we lack understanding of real love and loyalty, we treat them as cheap.

At the marriage alter and while looking in the eyes of their soon-to-be husband or wife, people have declared their unwavering love on their wedding day. Then, for various reasons, some couples walk away from their marriage vows. Those who once said, *"I will never leave you... I will never walk away; through sickness, through death, through good times and bad times, I will be here,"* are now divorcing. Over time, their love turned to hate. Today, unfortunately, over seventy percent of marriages end in divorce.

Again, this is reflective of the church. Many church members will confess their love and support; however, for various reasons, they eventually break their vows and divorce from that house of worship. When they do, they tend to be as hateful as the couples who once pledged their everlasting love.

Love, or God, is from everlasting to everlasting.

Before giving a platform, or position, to those who appear to be in agreement with the vision of the church, there needs to be an extensive qualification process in place. Look at this verse in 1 John:

"They went out from us, but they were not of us; for if they had been of us, they would have continued with us; but they went out that they might be made manifest, that none of them were of us." (1 John 2:19 NKJV)

If they were of us, they would have continued with us; and, them leaving was the proof they weren't of us. In the past, I spent days crying over those who left The Favor Life Church. However, it is important to clarify, not all who leave are of the spirit of Jezebel, nor are they all out of the will of God. For Pastors, it is necessary they understand, it is impossible to lead everyone who comes into their church. It is as they say, "Different strokes for different folks." At the same time, many who have left, or who have exited our lives, did so wrongly; thereby, resulting in deep wounds to the Kingdom of God, taking months to heal. Sadly, it almost always cuts the sheep who have become the wolf's prey. Thankfully, there is a day of reckoning for the sin of disloyalty and dissension. And, to stop these, we must die to our own human love and allow Love Himself to manifest, through us, to all men.

"Hell has no weapon against a person who decides Love is for everyone."

In Detroit, Michigan, on a ministry trip with my wife, God woke me up with His still, small voice stating, *"Hell has no weapon against a man who has decided to love everybody."* Man cannot fail when love rules over hate. I responded, *"Lord, I don't understand. Are you telling me to love?"* The Lord impressed upon me, *"Son, you decide to love; I cannot make you choose love. Love is your decision. To Love your enemy, son, you are going to have to possess my love within you, which is Christ's love."* **Through Christ in us, God's love is the only, real, way to stay loyal.**

After hearing God's words, I began to cry. I asked the Holy Spirit to help me forgive and release, from my heart, the offenses and wounds I had allowed others to place there; *"Lord, You are my Healer, and no one can remove these infractions but You."* At that moment, I began to heal. Too many times, we try to fix ourselves without addressing the heart. However, the truth is, healing begins from the inside out. And, to understand what's happening around us is to recognize what's going on within us.

WHY IS LOYALTY SO IMPORTANT?

- **Loyalty is the principal qualification for every person desiring to minister in the body of Christ.** *"Let a man so consider us, as servants of Christ and stewards of the mysteries of God. Moreover, it is required in stewards that one be found faithful."* (1 Corinthians 4:1-3 NKJV)
- **Loyalty will produce peace, and safety, in the local church.** Where there is a lack of loyalty, the atmosphere becomes agitated and aggressive. And, because sheep will not drink water when feeling unsafe, the rest of the church won't find water to drink in this environment.
- *Loyalty opens the door for the love of God to flow within the church.* "A new commandment I give to you, that you love one another; as I have loved you, that you also love one another. By this all will know that you are My disciples, if you have love for one another." (John 13:34-35 NKJV)
- **Loyalty is required to have a healthy ministry.**
- **Loyalty is required to have a long lasting, joyful ministry.**
- *Loyalty must be present, in our lives,* **in order to reap our full reward.** *"But you are those who have continued with Me in My trials. And I bestow upon you a kingdom, just as My Father bestowed one upon Me, that you may eat and drink at My table in My kingdom, and sit on thrones judging the twelve tribes of Israel."* (Luke 22:28-31 NKJV)

CHAPTER SIX

EIGHT STAGES OF DISLOYALTY

"Beware of false prophets, who come to you in sheep's clothing, but inwardly they are ravenous wolves. You will know them by their fruits. Do men gather grapes from thorn bushes or figs from thistles? Even so, every good tree bears good fruit, but a bad tree bears bad fruit. A good tree cannot bear bad fruit, nor can a bad tree bear good fruit. Every tree that does not bear good fruit is cut down and thrown into the fire. Therefore, by their fruits you will know them." (Matthew 7:15-20 NKJV)

Many, in our churches, start out excited about what God has planned for them, in their newly, found house of worship. However, after a while, those once enthusiastic people begin to wax cold. They start talking negatively about the church as well as the leadership they were once in love with.

In most churches and ministries, disloyalty is the number one killer. It has also ruined many marriages causing the faithful to become unfaithful. I have a problem with people who call themselves friend, or say they are connected, but sit in the enemy's presence feeling comfortable. Their words and their actions don't line up. Disloyal people can be worse than a thousand demons.

> **"Sometimes ministry just can't be nice."**

HOW TO DEAL WITH THE SPIRIT OF DISLOYALTY

- Become a discerner of spirits and correct those carrying wrong attitudes. Discernment is when the spirit tells you something your mind won't.

- Proper role modeling. Refrain from hobnobbing with the disloyal, otherwise, the sheep will do the same. Set the right example.
- Have a sheep-dog mentality. Protect the sheep from being kissed, or bitten. Remember, wolves don't come dressed as wolves, but as sheep.
- Stop tolerating the antics of a disloyal person. Immediately fire disloyalty...put an end to it. Because it is a heart issue, disloyal people always cry when they are caught. Don't mistake their tears of exposure as repentance.
- Don't give them a place of authority in the body.
- Avoid promoting people until their true character is proven.
- Mark those who cause division and avoid them. And, teach the people in your church to do the same. *"Now I urge you, brethren, note those who cause divisions and offenses, contrary to the doctrine which you learned, and avoid them. For those who are such do not serve our Lord Jesus Christ, but their own belly, and by smooth words and flattering speech deceive the hearts of the simple."* (Romans 16:17-18)
- Pray for them. *"Woe to you when all men speak well of you, For, so did their fathers to the false prophets. But I say to you who hear: Love your enemies, do well to those who hate you, bless those who curse you, and pray for those who spitefully use you."* (Luke 6:26-28)
- Leave vengeance to the Lord; their own pride will bring them down.

STAGE ONE: THE INDEPENDENT STAGE

This is the stage when the rules, of the group, no longer apply. The independent ones are those who think they are indispensable and can do what they want, say what they want, and come and go when they want.

Tardiness is silent rebellion; but, that doesn't stop them from being late, to most meetings, because they are full of excuses. They are never consistent in their commitments and are the ones who shout the loudest. While preaching regarding the actions of others, they are the ones who stand, proclaiming "Amen" the loudest. They regularly do what they want rather than what they are told; and, they interpret your instructions instead of following them. Unfortunately, though you would like for them to leave, they don't. They stay so they can spread their poison. And, they are the ones speaking against what is demanded of others. Expect stage two when trying to correct, or mentor, them.

STAGE TWO: THE OFFENSE STAGE

Jesus' disciples, basically, asked Him, "would You describe how You see the end of the age and the sign of Your coming?"

"Now as He sat on the Mount of Olives, the disciples came to Him privately, saying, "Tell us, when these things will be? And what will be the sign of your coming, and of the end of the age?" And Jesus answered and said to them: "Take heed that no one deceives you. For many will come in My name, saying, 'I am the Christ,' and will deceive many. And you will hear of wars and rumors of wars. See that you are not troubled; for all these things must come to pass, but the end is not yet. For nation will rise against nation, and kingdom against kingdom. And there will be famines, pestilences, and earthquakes in

various places. All these are the beginning of sorrows. Then they will deliver you up to tribulation and kill you, and you will be hated by all nations for My name's sake. **And, then, many will be offended**, *will betray one another, and will hate one another. Then many false prophets will rise up and deceive many. And because lawlessness will abound, the love of many will grow cold. But he who endures to the end shall be saved. And this gospel of the kingdom will be preached in all the world as a witness to all the nations, and then the end will come."* (Matthew 24:3-14 NKJV)

When Jesus was talking to the disciples about the end of the age and the sign of His return, He said, "there would be wars, and rumors of wars, pestilence, famine, sickness, etc." These have occurred throughout the ages and were described as "the beginning of sorrows," but they are not the end. However, the sign of the end was this... **"Many would be offended in that day... and would betray one another, and hate one another..."**

Never, in any generation, has there been so many court cases involving the most trivial and spiteful reasons. We see intolerance running rampant along with superficial forgiveness. Outwardly, as though they don't matter, we pretend to ignore another's actions; then, at the first opportunity, tell how we were offended. ***Sadly, this is not forgiveness.*** Because people tend to be pampered and spoiled, they can be easily annoyed with most everything. And, it is believed they have a right to say how annoyed they are. Sometimes it goes beyond offense to indignation. Statements such as, **"They shouldn't have done it that way; They should have had it ready; That shouldn't have been**

done this way, however, it should have been done this way; or, I don't like this," are reflective of an indignant attitude.

If the offense and indignation are not dealt with immediately, it could easily move into resentment; it is here that people remember *every time* an offense has occurred in their past. Their thoughts scream, *"It seems as though every time I go there, I get offended,"* or *"they acted like that the last time,"* and *"whaa, whaa, whaa..."* (Baby!)

The spirit of offense affects people daily, however, it is necessary to make the decision, "I am not going to be offended by people, words, or actions." This is possible by practicing: giving others the benefit of the doubt, showing tolerance, patience, and understanding, as well as, allowing for human imperfection. By building upon these, it is possible to enjoy being with people and appreciate their unique differences. You may even find you are amused at the very things that used to annoy you. Just remember, anything done consistently for twenty-one days becomes a habit. It takes effort to not be offended but, afterwards, it is well worth it.

The process of offense and indignation will be internalized if not dealt with; it will evolve into a **spirit of offense** which will become part of who you are. Eventually, the external effects of offense, reflected by your behavior, will determine how you perceive your world. Unfortunately, if it is not dealt with, the joy of life is stolen. At this stage, correction won't change the independent ones, it will offend them. It is here they become angry, hurt, and resentful, then, they disconnect from, and become disloyal to the ministry head.

STAGE THREE: THE UNINVOLVED STAGE

"Cursed is he who does the work of the Lord deceitfully, And, cursed is he who keeps back his sword from blood." (Jeremiah 48:10 NKJV)

Be aware of **uninvolved** people; individuals who start out sitting in the front but, now, sit in the back. They don't appear to listen and they lack interest in the vision of the house. And, when they speak, it is constant negativity. Fluctuating attendance, giving, and serving in the church are characteristic flaws of a disloyal person. It is imperative to keep "uninvolved" people from leadership positions in order to prevent divisiveness within the body. At this point, correcting or mentoring them comes with a *"whatever,"* or, *"stop bothering me"* attitude.

STAGE FOUR: THE CRITICAL STAGE

The uninvolved, or passive person, will almost always become critical; *"**Skepticism creates the greatest loss on earth.**"* Because criticism stops momentum, it is important to avoid people who criticize the vision of the house as well as the current leadership. Their MO is finding fault and is a dead give-away to discerning this type of person.

Every perceived thing is flawed which makes perfection an illusion. This means nothing, and no one, on earth is perfect. God left Himself out of everything on earth so that by people connecting to the earth, it wouldn't complete them. Jesus was, and is, the only source of perfection. Sadly, when the "uninvolved" discover the faults of others, they magnify them, making them bigger than they really are in order to prove themselves right.

Absalom saw David's faults without seeing his greatness or his anointing; nor did he recognize David's mercy or love. By all rights, Absalom should have been put to death for his actions against his half-brother, however, it was David's mercy that saved him. As it turned out, Absalom was only concerned about one thing, his promotion. This caused him to be critical about everything David did.

> **"Skepticism Creates the Greatest Loss on Earth."**

Critical people love talking to complainers, especially if the complaining is against the person they are disconnecting from. Most critical people don't understand, it was God who placed a particular person in the seat of authority within His house. So, to complain about His person, angers Him.

STAGE FIVE: THE POLITCAL STAGE

As a person becomes offended and begins to unplug from the ministry, complaining and criticizing becomes the norm. And, it is at this stage, like-minded people begin to join with them. Sadly, sometimes people who have not had negative issues with leadership, can lose confidence when they are presented with doubts, or questions, causing them to join with the dissenters.

Have you ever turned your blinker on while driving down interstate, confident in your decision to exit, when your passenger asks, *"Are you sure you want to take this exit?"* What happens? Immediately, you position your vehicle back into traffic while looking, at your passenger, saying, *"Yes, why? Do you know something that I don't?"* You were confident until someone questioned your decision. Then, regrettably, this doubt caused an unfortunate delay to your destination. The same can happen in our churches. There are people who know, without a shadow of a doubt, they belong in a particular church, until someone questions their loyalty. Then, their confidence is eroded and they begin to be critical and skeptical of leadership as well. Without taking responsibility, the disloyal insurrectionist begins playing politics in order to prove he is right.

"Now this I say lest anyone should deceive you with persuasive words. For though I am absent in the flesh, yet I am with you in spirit, rejoicing to see your good order and the steadfastness of your faith in Christ. As you therefore have received Christ Jesus the Lord, so walk in Him, rooted and built up in Him and established in the faith, as you have been taught, abounding in it with thanksgiving. Beware lest anyone cheat you through philosophy and empty deceit, according to the tradition of men, according to the basic principles of the world, and not according to Christ. For in Him dwells all the fullness of the Godhead bodily; and you are complete in Him, who is the head of all principality and power." (Colossians 2:4-10 NKJV)

"Now I urge you, brethren, note those who cause divisions and offenses, contrary to the doctrine which you learned, and avoid them. For those who are such do not serve our Lord Jesus Christ, but their own belly, and by smooth words and flattering speech deceive the hearts of the simple. For your obedience has become known to all. Therefore, I am glad on your behalf; but I want you to be wise in what is good, and simple concerning evil. And the God of

peace will crush Satan under your feet shortly." (Romans 16:17-20 NKJV)

The disloyal person will ask political questions in order to determine who will join in their coup. This is done by disguising their real identity and by asking loaded questions.

BAITED QUESTIONS, OR STATEMENTS

1. How did you find our services?
2. As a Bible-based church, do you think we should see more miracles?
3. Do you believe the pastor's focus has changed? He seems to be overly focused on *(fill in the blank)* and not souls.
4. Do you believe the pastor is as anointed as he was last year?
5. Have you noticed lots of people are leaving?
6. I think our pastor travels too much, don't you?
7. I sure liked the pastor, and his wife, better when the ministry was smaller, didn't you?
8. Do you think church services are too long?
9. I sure wish pastor wouldn't preach so hard.
10. Do you believe the pastor makes too much money?
11. The pastor seems to be more focused on the offering than the word of God.
12. Does the pastor's wife seem unfriendly?
13. Does the pastor shake your hand after church?
14. I don't like the songs we sing, do you?
15. There's too much emphasis on *(you fill in the blank)* and not enough on the word of God.
16. Everyone is saying... many people said this, or that. *The truth is no one said anything.*

17. Do you believe the pastor's children should be more spiritual?
18. Can you believe the pastors children sin?

STAGE SIX: THE DECEPTION STAGE

At this point, the insurrectionist is coming to a place he is unwilling to change; he has gotten caught up in his own lies and believe them to be truth.

"This I say, therefore, and testify in the Lord, that you should no longer walk as the rest of the Gentiles walk, in the futility of their mind, having their understanding darkened, being alienated from the life of God, because of the ignorance that is in them, because of the blindness of their heart; who, being past feeling, have given themselves over to lewdness, to work all uncleanness with greediness." (Ephesians 4:17-19 NKJV)

For nearly five-years, a couple attended the Favor Life Church then, for unknown reasons, abruptly left. For months, I sensed they were not acting right, however, they would not express, to me, what they were feeling. Multiple times I asked them if there was anything wrong, but their answer was always the same, *"No, we love you and the church."* Then, sometime after they left, I got an email stating, *"Bishop, we believe that God is done with us at The Favor Life Church. God has called us to be soul winners and we feel you are putting too much focus on television and not on evangelism... God has led us to move on..."* Needless to say, after the time spent pouring into their lives and praying for their success, this hurt.

Unfortunately, there was no evidence they evangelized anyone while at the Favor Life Church.

However, we have received many, many letters from people who have been touched, saved, helped, and delivered through the television ministry at this Church.

God, supposedly, led them to attend a Sunday, home group, where they leave their living room in order to sit at someone's kitchen table. Is that really "God leading them?" They left a church that offers amazing praise and worship, challenging preaching, and people who are equipped to help you grow and succeed. Now, they sit in someone's house, under someone who is not sanctioned, nor called by God, to lead them. Let me be clear, this is **not** the leading of the Holy Spirit.

People, at this stage, are self-vindicated. They are convinced the lies they have believed, are true; now, it is impossible to reach them. Sadly, not only will they continue to be deceived, but they will deceive others as well.

STAGE SEVEN: THE OPEN REBELLION STAGE

Having reached this stage, they are no longer in hiding; they openly fight leadership. Because of the confidence they have in their own deception and lies, they believe they are justified when they attack the pulpit. I've said it once, and I will say it again, "You haven't seen a good fight until you see a church fight."

STAGE EIGHT: EXECUTION STAGE

Together, with stage seven, the execution stage is created by the spirit of rebellion. This stage determines that an individual will rise up for the purpose of attacking the ministry head of the church.

Remember, rebellion is as the sin of witchcraft. It is imperative the church disarm every insurrectionist prior to reaching stages six, seven, and eight; otherwise, if they are not exposed, the hope for change diminishes. However, once they reach this level of rebellion, God sees them as witches, or devil worshippers. Exodus 22:18 says. *"Thou shall not suffer a witch to live!"* God expects the church to destroy this spirit. Open rebellion against the leadership of the church is satanic; not of God. He would never rise up against those He has placed in authority.

"For there is no authority except from God, and the authorities that exist are appointed by God. Therefore, whoever resists the authority resists the ordinance of God and those who resist will bring judgment on themselves. For rulers are not a terror to good works, but to evil. Do you want to be unafraid of the authority? Do what is good, and you will have praise from the same. For he is God's minister to you for good. But if you do evil, be afraid; for he does not bear the sword in vain; for he is God's minister, an avenger to execute wrath on him who practices evil. Therefore, you must be subject, not only because of wrath but also for conscience' sake. For because of this you also pay taxes, for they are God's ministers attending continually to this very thing." (Romans 13:1-7 NKJV)

The church must submit to delegated authority. It is not a democracy because that way of thinking does not work within the governmental structure of the church. Its mind-set must line-up with the Kingdom of God; a mind-set that understands Jesus is the King of the Kingdom we call church. Whoever King Jesus places in authority now speaks, and leads, for Him. When someone attacks His designated leader, that attack is, actually, against the King. Even Michael, the Archangel, wouldn't rise up against God's delegated authority.

"Likewise, also these dreamers defile the flesh, reject authority, and speak evil of dignitaries. Yet Michael the archangel, in contending with the devil, when he disputed about the body of Moses, dared not bring against him a reviling accusation, but said, "The Lord rebuke you!" But these speak evil of whatever they do not know; and whatever they know naturally, like brute beasts, in these things they corrupt themselves. Woe to them! For they have gone in the way of Cain, have run greedily in the error of Balaam for profit, and perished in the rebellion of Korah." (Jude 8-11 NKJV)

Do you see what was said through the Word of the Lord? He stated, "these dreamers defile the flesh, reject authority, and speak evil of persons of high rank, or office." There is a fine line between the Freedom of Speech and the freedom to say what you want. If your speech damages, or hurts, those in high-ranking positions, it is wrong! Words are sharp weapons and, when used against someone, can create wounds that take years to heal.

In America, due to Freedom of Speech, it is disgusting how people, and the media, are allowed to talk about, or against, the President of the United States; against all those granted authority through the election process. We have no right to attack any leader with words that can hurt them. It doesn't matter if they are republican, democrat, or independent. In my opinion, this has gotten out of control because the church has digressed, or wandered away from respect, into disrespect, in this area as well. It is said, "As the church goes, so goes the world." So, when the church disrespects God's appointed leaders, expect the world to grow worse.

People, at this stage, are deceived into believing they are operating according to the spirit of the Lord. However, they are not; they have been totally deceived. They are now, what I believe to be, unreachable...not capable of being mentored. There are many, in that day, who will be deceived saying, *"Lord, Lord,"* however, Jesus warned us that He does not know such people.

WOLVES IN SHEEP CLOTHING

If Lucifer, or any of his demons, entered the church in order to take it over and throw out the appointed leader, I believe the congregation would rise up, rebuke them, and cast them out of the church, or local body. Nobody wants to see the enemy ruin our churches, or our pastors, however, too often this is exactly what happens. Board members rise up, congregants rise up, and staff members rise up against the appointed leader ready to cast them down, and throw them out.

In my time, I have witnessed some terrible church fights happen in the name of the Lord. I've watched as men began facing off with the man of God fully intent on fighting him. These are supposed to be spirit-filled, anointed men who are there to lift up and support the pulpit, not destroy it; this is an atrocity to the church.

"Beware of false prophets, who come to you in sheep's clothing, but inwardly they are ravenous wolves. You

will know them by their fruits." (Matthew 7:15-16 NKJV)

Wolves travel in packs; they are never alone. They will always send one of their own to infiltrate the flock of sheep. And, this wolf will even crawl under the skin of a dead sheep in order to get as close as it can. No flock would ever, intentionally, allow a wolf to get near them so, how does this happen? The sheep get caught up in feeding and grazing and they lose focus on what's going on around them. The wolf, wearing the dead sheep skin, appears to be like them, so they are not afraid. However, the deceptively, disguised wolf is there to do them harm. As it gets closer, it bites a sheep's hind leg, crippling it. Because it trusted a wolf in sheep's clothing, the once healthy sheep is now weakened. Then, as the shepherd leads the flock to the next pasture, or season, the wounded ones have a problem keeping up; they begin falling further and further behind. Then, once they are alone, the wolves devour them. This is the same pattern the enemy will use to deceive the people in our churches. Satan knows we would never allow him in the church, so he sends a person (wolf), dressed in sheep's clothing, in order to get close.

"For I know this, that after my departure savage wolves will come in among you, not sparing the flock. Also, from among yourselves men will rise up, speaking perverse things, to draw away the disciples after themselves. Therefore watch, and remember that for three years I did not cease to warn everyone night and day with tears." (Acts 20:29-31 NKJV)

Within the church, there needs to be more vigilance against such people. A diligence that prevents the wolves from getting close to the growing and changing sheep as well as those who are attempting to fit in. The job of the shepherd is to watch over the sheep, night and day; guarding and staying focused on the flock. He makes sure the sheep are grazing safely and fellowshipping without confusion or strife, so they can partake of all that's necessary for maturity. God never intended for us, as leaders, to allow insurrectionists to ruin, or control, what He is endeavoring to do through them. Leaders are not to sit in the back of the church, allowing anything, or anyone, to come into His house for the purpose of causing harm to the people.

"Woe to the worthless shepherd, who leaves the flock! A sword shall be against his arm and against his right eye; His arm shall completely wither, and his right eye shall be totally blinded." (Zechariah 11:17 NKJV)

CHAPTER SEVEN

SIGNS OF DISLOYALTY

Disloyalty, a secret weapon the enemy uses to destroy organizations from within; their goal is to find an individual who has become disgruntled with authority. Remember, it will almost always be the person chosen, by leadership, to lead. After becoming angry, they begin actively resisting the pastor as well as the other leaders. Then, they establish a following of angry, dissatisfied people who instigate hideous battles against the head of the organization. Those, in opposition, seem to believe they are being led by the Spirit of God, which is ridiculous. Disloyalty is a process that takes time but, eventually, people will stand against the person in charge in order to destroy them with their words.

40 SIGNS OF DISLOYALTY

1. *People who have moral weaknesses you cannot correct.* People who struggle with moral issues will hide them for as long as they can. However, eventually, those issues will be revealed because they begin acting, overly, holy. When their moral purity begins to break down, they tend to be excessively critical of other people dealing with their own moral struggles. Unfortunately, correcting a person in this condition is impossible. Never the less, their guilt is exposed through the anger they express when questioned about their morality.

2. *People with poor Financial Habits.* God gave laws that decide financial increase; He doesn't give money. People with bad, financial, habits can become prime candidates of disloyalty. If they can't

manage their finances, they will struggle to manage those placed under their authority. It is true, money can reveal a person's character flaws. And, if it were God who decided where the money goes, why does the mafia have it rather than missionaries? Because the universe is run by God's laws, obeyed, or disobeyed, they decide the money people have.

3. *People who think they know more and can lead better.* Many people are smarter than I am, however, those who believe I can't teach or lead them, will sever their connection and go other places. They will begin interjecting their own thoughts rather than listening to the mentorship they are given. It is necessary to immediately silence them in order to keep the door open for a healthy relationship.

4. *People who have never recovered from woundedness.* Wounded people will come into our congregations who refuse to be corrected. Because they were wounded in another congregation, and need to be healed, they are not ready to be placed in any type of leadership role. The cost of doing so, could result in immense difficulty. So, prior to advancing anyone in this condition, give them time to heal, time to forgive, and time to let go of their previous, ministry wounds.

5. *People not willing to be trained, or retrained.* They will use words like, "*I know... I know; I've been in ministry for years.*" When attending meetings, bring a notepad, be ready to listen and learn. Otherwise, this makes it obvious

they are not interested in learning what you know.

6. ***People who constantly proclaim their credentials.*** For years, a person on my staff would, constantly, tell people of all their titles and accomplishments. At first, I thought they were proud of all they had done, however, in the end, they had a hidden agenda. Eventually, they left the Favor Life ministry in order to start their own.

7. ***People who refuse to do menial jobs.*** Be aware of the people who declare, "that's not in my job description." Sometimes, as a test, I leave trash laying around while watching to see who will pick it up. I have determined that, those who see the trash, but don't pick it up, may have problems serving others.

8. ***A person constantly at war with their spouse.*** Marriage takes commitment and is the breeding ground where loyalty and commitment are proven. When married couples, especially in leadership, are always fighting, this could be a sign they could turn on you.

9. ***People who get irritated and have wrong reactions when corrected.*** Correction decides connection. The quality of a leader will be in proportion to their ability to take correction. If those under authority will not allow ministry heads to correct them, distance yourself and be prepared to remove them from leadership. Watch out for people who are easily offended; for, the offended heart can become bitter and poisoned.

10. ***People who make excuses then justify***

themselves when in error.

11. ***People who do not keep their promises.*** It is wise to do a credit check on the people you surround yourself with. If the person's credit score is terrible, it could mean, they are not good at keeping their promises. Of course, this is not always the case; do your research before judging. You can also do background checks to promote greater confidence as the ministry, or business, is growing.

12. ***People who constantly lobby for promotion, or recognition.*** Some people live life with false expectation on how others should treat them. They expect to be complimented, or recognized, over the smallest things. Though they may be a paid staff member, they act as though they are serving instead of working. Their need for compliments and recognition could indicate they have insecurities, or a wound of rejection. They, typically, disappoint themselves as well as others. When false, or overly high, expectation, is placed on someone, the result can lead to a season of disappointment. Deferred hope makes the heart sick and can cause the person to become critical.

13. ***People who are rarely criticized, or corrected, such as amateur, or young leaders.*** It is not that young people can't lead but they can be easily distracted. This happens because they haven't, truly, learned how to be loyal. Taking the time to train young leaders is key for everyone's success.

14. ***Someone not attentive, taking notes, or***

uninvolved during teaching and preaching. People, who are connected, will want to hear what is being taught, or preached. However, a leader who seems disinterested could cause problems in the future. Their lack of interest could indicate having picked up an offense regarding the ministry head. Now, they are not interested in learning from them.

15. *People who do not help other ministry departments succeed.* Non-team-players are prime candidates for insurrection. I want people who are concerned for all areas of the church, not just their own place of ministry.

16. *People who do not tithe or sow into the ministry, or ministry head.* I could write pages on this because, if people are not willing to give of their money, they will never be loyal. To Bible believers, tithing is a no-brainer. If leadership is not tithing, it is necessary they be, immediately, corrected. Then, if they still refuse to tithe, sit them down. Sadly, people who do not tithe are under a curse; living in poverty and sickness. And, anyone they are connected to could be affected by that same curse.

17. *People who, consistently, miss regular meetings.* It is understood people sometimes miss ministry meetings, or gatherings, due to work, illness, or being out of town; however, it is important to monitor inconsistency in attendance. This is especially true for special events, or meetings. During midweek services I, generally, watch people's attendance, then, listen for their reasons for not being there. Personally, I have seen

people who, regularly, miss services become disloyal when I would not allow them to step into leadership positions.

18. **People who are approving of those who make wrong decisions.** Due to the fact that wrong decisions can create a season of wrong consequences, this one gets my blood boiling. Experience is a great teacher; however, it is counterproductive to bail people out of their consequences while they are being trained in them. It makes the helper out to be an enemy of God and it also hinders leadership.

19. **People who poison, or try to poison, how someone thinks about others.** This one is self-explanatory. If a serpent is allowed in leadership, then, it should be expected that it will bite and poison others. Unfortunately, snakes do not sit silently but, instead, spew their poison on those who listen; most refuse to shut-up. Killing the snake, or removing the person from leadership and, if necessary, the church, is the only way to deal with this problem.

20. **People who will not mingle or interact with others.** Loners either have problems with themselves or with people. And, individuals who never mingle, or never interact with others, usually have internal damage which will, eventually, reveal itself. A growing ministry demands its leaders mingle.

21. **People who have a controlling spouse.** How a person interacts with their spouse is a reflection of the interaction they have with others. If a

married person won't stand up to their spouse when they are wrong, or out of order, then it is unlikely they will stand up for the ministry head when hard decisions have to be made.
- Once, a pastor friend asked his board members to refrain from spending time with, or counseling, a person who left the ministry with hatred; this individual also discredited the church as well as the senior pastor. Afterwards, one of the board member's wives stated, *"You're asking me to disobey the Lord. The Lord has directed me to counsel this person."* First of all, God does not ask people to do anything without the direction of the ministry head. This particular woman was controlling and did not like being told what to do. When the pastor informed me of the situation, as his bishop, I told him, "She was out of order and, if she didn't want to line-up then let the line out." That's exactly what happened, the board member, and his wife, left. Then, the ministry was able to come together in unity as well as church business.

22. **People who consistently shift the blame on others.** A person who consistently states their failures are someone else's fault has a real problem. Unteachable people are, generally, the ones who shift blame to others. Their wounds of rejection prevent them from facing their mistakes in order to fix them.

23. **People who think the senior pastor makes too much money.** If you Know someone who believes this sow, **"7 Strategic Prayers You Should Pray Over Your Pastor,"** into their life.

24. People who are not team players. Team players are important; there is no room in leadership for individuality.

25. People who are comfortable in your enemy's presence. If a person is comfortable with the ministry's enemies, then, they are probably in agreement with their opinion regarding leadership. I have a problem with people who claim to be our friends, or who are leaders in the church, but sit with those who attack the ministry head as well as the church. When confronted they state, *"Well, I'm just being Christ like."* Unfortunately, the truth is, they are being disloyal.

26. People who never pick a side. This goes along with number twenty-five. At one time, I had a staff person who, no matter what happened, would never really pick a side. However, in ministry, you are either on the ministry head's side or you're not. And, the ministry can't be divided in times of war because, "A house that is divided will fall." I have discovered that people will go to a person who refuses to take a side and complain about the vision of the church and myself. Rather than defending me, they would tell their complainers to pray. One example of this came after our secretary realized the deposit was different than the count. So, she questioned one of our staff members and wanted to know why. After shrugging their shoulders, the response seemed to be, *"Well, I don't know."* However, it would have been more appropriate to have informed the secretary of the intended purpose for the money not deposited. As a result, this gave the secretary the impression I was taking money out of the offering bag. Please, fire anyone who refuses to pick a side; and, it is preferable to pick the side of the ministry head.

27. People who act super-spiritual. Come on, you know all about these people; they claim everything is supernatural or spiritual. Give me a break!

28. People who consistently say they have a word from God. After the book of Malachi, God went silent for four-hundred years; however, it now seems, He can't stop talking. Most people claiming to have a word from God, instead, speak from their own mind. And, regarding His house and the direction of the church, before speaking to anyone else, God will speak to the ministry head first.

29. People who are comfortable with the ungodly. God calls people to witness and bring salvation to the ungodly; not hang out with them. The Word states that light has nothing in common with darkness. So, someone who is comfortable hanging out in darkness, probably hasn't fully committed to the things of God. They have yet to choose a side. (*Reference #26*)

30. People who trivialize what others feel is important.

31. People who believe they are owed something. People who believe they are entitled, walk in resentment toward leaders. No matter what anyone does, they believe they are owed something.

32. People who complain about others and

also about the ministry head in his absence. Some people will, consistently, complain about others as well as the ministry head. They are blinded to their own behaviors but can pin point the negative things someone else is doing, or not doing. It is important to be cautious when allowing a complainer to hang out with you. God despises complainers!

33. People who won't speak up in an argument or let their vote be counted. I once had a board member who, no matter what was being discussed within our meetings, would never say anything. Because this person sat quietly, I took his silence as agreement. However, this was not true; I've learned, the ones in agreement will always speak up.

34. People who will not follow instructions. Delayed obedience is disobedience. God doesn't bless a person who is in disobedience.

35. People with hidden agendas. No matter how committed a person is to serving, they will eventually leave if they have a hidden agenda. And, they usually leave in the wrong way. God's servants will serve because that is who they are, however, someone with a hidden agenda is not sent by God but by their own ambition. They are driven by their own agenda and desire for promotion.

36. People who are overly flirtatious. Men, "Watch out for flirtatious women." Disloyalty is the end-result when giving in to this temptation; wives and children will be hurt. And, there is no room for this in the Kingdom of God. I believe Satan sends flirtatious women into churches in order to distract the man of God. It is vital that men not share their family problems with anyone of the opposite sex; otherwise, bonds may be created resulting in even more problems.

37. *People who cause frustration during, and after, great attacks.* Selfish people are more concerned about their needs being met than about the needs of their leaders. They are not able to discern that their leader may have, just, come out of a season of attack. Therefore, to leaders, selfish people can be very frustrating. And, because frustration can create seasons of wrong decisions, leaders should be careful around them. For, when the waters within a ministry, or business, get rough, selfish people will not stick around. Frustration is a distraction and it weakens one's focus and robs them of their faith.

38. *People who are jealous of another's promotions.* Jealousy is the offspring of bitterness. First of all, jealous people, usually, don't believe in themselves. Second, many are wounded and tend to focus on what other people have rather than what they are capable of achieving.

39. *People who will not give praise and worship in the gathering.* I've seen this time and time again. In the beginning of the Favor Life Church, several of the leaders would sit through the services without worshiping, praising, or lifting their hands to God. When I would ask them *why*, they would respond with lame excuses. One, in particular, would cross his arms when the music minister would instruct the congregation to lift

their hands. His response when asked why was, *"No man is going to tell me what to do..."*

40. **People who are consistently depressed and have no joy.** Individuals who stay depressed are hard to reach and, eventually, become lost in the movement of the organization.

I know this list seems overwhelming, however, it will be worth your time, and effort, to learn these signs in order to teach them. It is important to understand, it is not impossible to minister healing to a person showing signs of disloyalty. Nevertheless, the mistake is made when the ministry head ignores what needs to be addressed; this can prove to be fatal to the ministry, or business involved. Be diligent to address, and teach, these signs. Instruct the team to expose anyone showing signs, or symptoms, of disloyalty. It is important, for everyone involved, to work together in order to clean up God's house.

CHAPTER EIGHT

WHY YOU NEED A PASTOR

And I will give you shepherds according to my heart, who will feed you with knowledge and understanding. "Then it shall come to pass, when you are multiplied and increased in the land in those days," says the Lord, "that they will say no more, 'The ark of the covenant of the Lord.' It shall not come to mind, nor shall they remember it, nor shall they visit it, nor shall it be made anymore. "At that time Jerusalem shall be called The Throne of the Lord, and all the nations shall be gathered to it, to the name of the Lord, to Jerusalem. No more shall they follow the dictates of their evil hearts." (Jeremiah 3:15-17 NKJV)

WHY WE NEED A PASTOR

God told us there would be a day when the Ark of the Covenant would not be needed; He would provide shepherds. The pastor, therefore, became the Ark's replacement on the battlefield. And, in order to fully understand the power and importance of the pastor, there are some key issues that need to be understood regarding the Ark of the Covenant. The Ark was the place where God housed His presence and His power; His power was hidden in His presence. It was made of acacia wood and covered in pure gold. Cut down the middle, and opened up, you would see layers of gold, then wood, then gold.

In the Bible, gold represents the Godhead while the wood represents humanity. Acacia wood is the hardest wood known to man; it will not rot. It is a type of Christ, in that, when Christ died, corruption could not touch him. The layers of gold, wood, and gold signified that Jesus, the Messiah, would come from deity, enter humanity and, then, return to deity. So, in the Old Covenant, the Ark of the Covenant was a type of Christ. However, in Jeremiah, God reveals that He will now place His assignments on man and the Ark would not be necessary. Now, the pastor, a type of the Ark, is raised upon the platform of the church, sitting above the people in order to protect them from the wolves who sneak in unaware. The platform is not a place of entertainment, but a battlefield in which the pastor has been prepared to destroy the thief who comes to steal, kill, and destroy.

CONTENT OF THE ARK

"Then indeed, even the first covenant had ordinances of divine service and the earthly sanctuary. For a tabernacle was prepared: the first part, in which was the lamp stand, the table, and the showbread, which is called the sanctuary; and behind the second veil, the part of the tabernacle which is called the Holiest of All, which had the golden censer and the ark of the covenant overlaid on all sides with gold, **in which were the golden pot that had the manna, Aaron's rod that budded, and the tablets of the covenant; and above it were the cherubim of glory overshadowing the mercy seat."** (Hebrews 9:1-5 NKJV)

God designed the Ark to have two cherubim angels, on top, whose wings touched each other; they covered and overshadowed the Ark. There were three types of angels in heaven:

- **Archangels**: Classified as principalities, or protectors of nations.
- **Seraphim**: They stand above the Lord singing,

"Holy, Holy, Holy is the Lord." They are the guardians of God's atmosphere.
- **Cherubim**: They stand for the power of knowing, and beholding, God. They are filled with divine wisdom which is poured out through them. Genesis 25:22 states that, "From between the Cherubim," God would commune with Moses.

The Spirit of Wisdom overshadows true pastors even as the Cherubim overshadow the Ark of the Covenant. And, "Between the Cherubim" is where the Wisdom of God communes with pastors. It is important to note, the Cherubim also cover the mercy seat. God's mercy is strongest when people are connected to the five-fold ministry which is overshadowed by the Wisdom of God. Because of this, Satan knows that seasons of loss and pain are created when individuals disconnect from the man/woman of God.

INSIDE THE ARK

1. Golden pot of manna
2. Aaron's rod that budded
3. The broken tablets of the covenant

The senior pastor is the container of God's mantle, His message, and His miracles; these assignments are not possible without God's appointed messengers. There has to be a covenant connection to the man of God.

THE MANTLE

The mantle is God's calling, or His holy

selection upon the man of God; it is the manna, the breath of God placed in the mouth of the pastor. The gathering of the church is where the manna is fed to the children of God. He rains down the Word of God upon those who will hear.

There was a system to the manna falling upon the earth; first, the dew would cover the earth, then the manna. Afterwards, the children of Israel would collect just enough for their daily bread. *"And when the dew fell on the camp in the night, the manna fell on it."* (Numbers 11:9 NKJV) Here, the earth represents the flesh, the dew represents the Spirit of God, and the manna represents God's spoken word. So, without the Holy Spirit first covering the ground, the Word of God (manna) would not have had anything to connect to and would not have been able to sustain the Israelites.

However, for forty-years, the children of Israel ate the manna; they survived in a wilderness that would have otherwise killed them. Miraculously, their shoes never wore out, their clothes never wore out and, their bodies never became sick. Because they ate the manna, their belongings were also protected.

It was necessary for the dew, or the Spirit of God, to first be applied on the ground, or the flesh. Today, when there is praise and worship being offered to the Father, the Spirit of the Lord falls upon man's flesh. In this atmosphere, God inhabits the people's praise. *"But thou art holy, O thou that inhabits the praises of Israel."* (Psalm 22:3) He sends the Spirit to hover over man and, then, He fills them. God's presence is the one place where our weaknesses die.

As the ministry head, when we gather for worship service, I pay attention to those who are not worshipping; they tend to be bothered by those participating and are unable to receive the word being preached. Due to a lack of worship, the Word, or manna, is not retained and it prevents the people from being wet with the dew of God's Spirit. If this process is ignored, people can expect everything in their lives to break down or wear out. This includes marriages, minds, health, jobs, and finances; all are attached to the receiving, and eating, of the manna. No worship, no rain. No rain (dew), no manna.

THE MESSAGE

*"For since, in the wisdom of God, the world through wisdom did not know God, it pleased God through the foolishness of **the message** preached to save those who believe."* (1 Corinthians 1:21-22 NKJV)

*"But the Lord stood with me and strengthened me, so **that the message might be preached** fully through me, and that all the Gentiles might hear. Also, I was delivered out of the mouth of the lion. And the Lord will deliver me from every evil work and preserve me for His heavenly kingdom. To Him be glory forever and ever. Amen!"* (2 Timothy 4:17-18 NKJV)

The broken tablets, containing God's ten-commandments, represent the power of His message. His laws are hidden within the heart of every anointed preacher, or those called to be in the five-fold ministry. They came into the body of Christ broken, but have been made whole by the blood of the lamb in order to do ministry. By the Holy Spirit, the pastor is the voice of conviction, empowerment, and love. And, the Spirit of wisdom is given, enabling people to change in His presence. The messenger's voice carries power to also change cities and nations. And, just as Moses, in a time of battle, needed believers to help hold his arms up, today God's messengers need the same.

"How then shall they call on Him in whom they have not believed? And how shall they believe in Him of whom they have not heard? And how shall they hear without a preacher? And how shall they preach unless they are sent?" (Romans 10:14-15 NKJV)

The pastor carries the message, or instruction, to be preached so others can hear and be changed. Without shepherds, present seasons could become permanent due to a lack of the proper directions necessary for change to occur. God always calls on man to be a vessel for the declaration of His word; and, as an instrument to reveal His works of power to others. It would be wise to refrain from wickedly touching, attacking, or even talking about the man God has chosen for His purposes.

THE MIRACLE

The man of God carries, within himself, the power of a miracle. I believe, when the person God has selected for governmental order is in position, the atmosphere is pregnant with the budding rod of Aaron. This is a spiritual phenomenon! Because the rod of Aaron was cut from the root of a tree, in all perspectives, it was a dead piece of wood. It was cut off from its source of life, therefore, it lost its power to reproduce, grow, or change. However, Aaron's rod produced buds and showed signs of life every year. And, because it had no root system, this was far from normal. That's the miracle of the pastor. When people hear the ministry of the Word of life, just like the rod, it creates the miracle of new growth so that change can take place. So, when the pastor, truly, represents the Ark of the Covenant, the enemy flees from the battle he is waging against the people.

"So, it was whenever the ark set out, that Moses said: "Rise up, O Lord! Let Your enemies be scattered, And, let those who hate You flee before You." (Numbers 10:35 NKJV)

"But they presumed to go up to the mountaintop. Nevertheless, neither the ark of the covenant of the Lord nor Moses departed from the camp. Then the Amalekites and the Canaanites who dwelt in that mountain came down and attacked them, and drove them back as far as Hormah." (Numbers 14:44-45 NKJV)

    The reverence, of the people, towards the Ark of the Covenant, or the presence of God, put fear in the hearts of their enemies. I believe a pastor can invoke the same fear today. When the body of Christ begins to recognize the presence of God within the pastor, then praise and worship of the Lord will come forth. As this takes place, the enemy will leave the battlefield because he fears the power of God. And, with the presence of God advancing towards the enemy, the people of God have a sense of praise, and of joy. A true pastor, led of the Spirit, can manifest this same outcome. So, when the enemy recognizes the connection between the carrier of God's presence and the people of God, he will fear the battlefield.

    Unfortunately, when the children of Israel sinned, the presence of God did not show up; it was their guilt that stopped the movement of the Ark which resulted in great loss. The same can be said of our churches. Today, when people stop listening to truth and begin disrespecting the pastor due to rejection, or offense, they stop bringing him to the battlefield. Therefore, God's presence is not there to help and, the result is the same, LOSS! Loss of land... Loss of finances... Loss of friends and family... and, in some cases, loss of life.

"And, when the ark of the covenant of the Lord came into the camp, all Israel shouted so loudly that the earth shook. Now when the Philistines heard the noise of the shout, they said, "What does the sound of this great shout in the camp of the Hebrews mean?" Then they understood that the ark of the Lord had come into the camp. So, the Philistines were afraid, for they said, "God has come into the camp!" And they said, "Woe to us!" (1 Samuel 4:5-7 NKJV)

Sadly, many people believe the pastor is a hireling; a person who works only for pay. He is brought in, by the deacons, to motivate and encourage the church. So, they believe, with enough votes, he can be fired if they don't like what he stands for. Unfortunately, a lot of pastors' families have been ruined as a result of this wrong understanding. And, because the congregation believed they were hired, instead of appointed by God, they took it upon themselves to become the pastor's employer, his judge, and his jury. God never gave this right, or authority, to any deacon, or congregation; however, He placed the government of His house upon the senior pastor. And, I had a good friend tell me, "The government of God will always produce the glory of God. The glory of God will always create the gold in the house." Increase, and money, are attached to our reaction to His appointed man of God.

Over time, I witnessed the mean and cruel treatment this wrong attitude inflicted upon the man of God. I, definitely, wouldn't want to be in their shoes on the day of judgment. On that day, the wrath of God is stored up for the wicked treatment of His five-fold ministry.

Death comes to those who wrongly touch the Ark. Look at the story below. When Uzzah put his hand upon the Ark, the anger of the Lord was aroused, and he was punished. Unfortunately, punishment is waiting for those who wrongly touch, through word or deed, His anointed ones.

"And when they came to Nachon's threshing floor, Uzzah put out his hand to the ark of God and took hold of it, for the oxen stumbled. Then the anger of the Lord was aroused against Uzzah, and God struck him there for his error; and he died there by the ark of God. And David became angry because of the Lord's outbreak against Uzzah; and he called the name of the place Perez Uzzah to this day. David was afraid of the Lord that day; and he said, "How can the ark of the Lord come to me?" So, David would not move the ark of the Lord with him into the City of David; but David took it aside into the house of Obed-Edom the Gittite. The ark of the Lord remained in the house of Obed-Edom the Gittite three months. And the Lord blessed Obed-Edom and all his household." (2 Samuel 6:1-11 NKJV)

Supernaturally, Aaron's rod would bud; though it was disconnected from its original source, it would bud because it was connected to a new source. To His sheep, God made pastors a source for miracles. Don't be discouraged if you had to walk away from friends, or family, in order to stay connected to a local church with an anointed pastor. Though you had to walk away from what once was, God will cause you to bud as well. And, as you remain connected to this new source, incredible miracles will be produced for you. So, no matter what, stay connected; this activates God's mercy seat.

According to Dictionary.com, a follower is a person who follows another in regard to his or her ideas or belief; he is a disciple or adherent. For me, I believe there are four different types of followers:

- ***The passive follower*** only reaches when it is convenient, or when their personal efforts do not produce their desired result. They, subconsciously, expect the pastor, as well as the church, to produce success for them.

- ***The parasite follower*** pursues for credibility, not for correction. They use the name and influence of a church, or pastor, to manipulate others into a relationship. The parasite wants what the pastor has earned through experience, not what he has learned; they want reputation without preparation.

- ***The prodigal follower*** enters and exits the relationship freely. But when serious correction is needed, they leave for another church, because the pastor, or congregation, does not know them or their flaws. The prodigal will distance themselves when a pastor, or the church, experiences personal attacks, difficulties, loss of credibility, false accusation, or persecution. However, the prodigal will return when their pigpen has become unbearable.

- ***The productive follower*** has a servant's heart. They never make a major decision without the counsel and feedback of their pastor. The productive follower views their pastor, and church, as a gift from God; they love their pastor as they love themselves. And, they view their connection as a divine privilege by God.

TEN SIGNS OF A PRODUCTIVE FOLLOWER

1. **Productive followers invest everything in order to stay in the presence of their pastor and church.**
2. **Follow the counsel of their pastor.**
3. **Reveal their secrets and dreams with the pastor of their church.**
4. **Freely discuss their mistakes and their pain with their pastor.**
5. **Clearly define their expectations to their pastor.**
6. **Gladly sow seeds of appreciation into the life of their pastor.**
7. **Receives the mantle of the pastor he serves.**
8. **During a season of warfare, will move toward the shelter of the pastor.**
9. **Will change their schedule in order to invest their time with the pastor.**
10. **Discerns, respects, and pursues the answers God has stored, within the pastor, for their life.** [i]

Closing Thoughts

I hope this study makes it clear how the body of Christ can recognize, and deal with, the people the enemy sends for the purpose of dividing, then destroying, what God has intended to build in others. This is not a manual for a "witch hunt"; it is not meant to hang, or burn, those who are different.

Being mature, being a Christian, and walking in love will help the axe of leadership to be received better. We must all stand against false prophets, the untrainable, the unteachable, and those who fight change. However, I will caution you, not everyone who fights, or resists, change is a disloyal person; they are, more than likely, scared. They lack the one, necessary, ingredient to make them better: ***COURAGE!***

- **IT TAKES COURAGE TO CHANGE.**
- **IT TAKES COURAGE TO ADMIT YOU NEED CHANGE.**
- **IT TAKES COURAGE TO TRY SOMETHING DIFFERENT.**
- **IT TAKES COURAGE TO BE CORRECTED AND CHOOSE TO STAY CONNECTED.**

The reason so many in our churches stay the same is because they lack courage to change. But, in order for someone to change, the need for something more must be recognized; their marriage needs more, their finances need more, they need more. However, replacing selfishness and pride with giving and humility is the change necessary for a better marriage, or a better ability to manage finances. Change is the ingredient that makes anyone, or anything, better.

After reading this book, it takes courage to admit to having been used as a disloyal insurrectionist; it might be hard to swallow, but probably true. By being honest with ourselves, we are able to see how we have talked about our leaders as well as our pastors. We have actively participated in insurrection by listening to others talk against, or watching others destroy, what leaders are working to build. Fortunately, this doesn't make a person an insurrectionist. An insurrectionist will continue talking against leadership. They are full of bitterness and anger which causes a hardening of their heart, making correction and change difficult. Unfortunately, in this condition, they are set up to be used by the enemy.

It is never a good idea to allow your mind to wander into a place that prevents discussing, with your leaders, the things hurting or troubling you.

No one can stay in one place forever. So, when you sense your time is up in the house you have been serving, seek the Lord first. Then, go straight to your pastor in order to inform him. Here is a word to the wise, "If God is done with you in one place, He will already be opening the door for the next place." God will never send you down the ladder, He will always send you up for mentorship and training.

It is important to allow the man of God to create a proper exodus for you; being "sent" is more powerful than jumping ship. Never leave hurt and never leave mad. And, make sure the Lord is really sending you rather than being stirred up by a discontented person. Disgruntled people try to persuade others to feel what they're feeling because, as the saying goes, "Misery loves company."

My prayer is that this book will help to bring

healing to those who have been hurt by the insurrectionist spirit. I am confident that its teachings will help slow down the wrong influence of others as well as help keep unity in the local church. Thank you for reading this book and becoming my partner in this endeavor. And, because of my love and passion for writing, you make it worthwhile for me to continue.

Dr. G

Decision Page

May I Invite You to Make Jesus Christ the Lord of Your Life?

The Bible says, *"That if you will confess with your mouth the Lord Jesus and will believe in your heart that God raised Him from the dead, you will be saved. For with the heart man believes unto righteousness; and with the mouth confession is made for salvation."* (Romans 10:9-10)

Pray this prayer with me today:
"Dear Jesus, I believe that You died for me and You rose again on the third day. I confess, to You, that I am a sinner. I need Your love and Your forgiveness. Come into my life, forgive my sins, and give me eternal life. I, now, confess You as my Lord. Thank You for my salvation! I will walk in Your peace and joy from this day forward. Amen!"

Signed_____

—

Date_____

—

[Mail this to Dr. Grillo]

☐ Yes, Dr. Jerry! I made a decision to accept Christ as my personal Lord and Savior today. And, I would like to be put on your mailing list.

Name

_____

Address

_____

City _____ State _____ Zip

_____ Phone _____ Email

_____

Fogzone Ministries
P.O. Box 3707, Hickory N.C. 28603
828.325.4773 Fax: 828.325.4877 www.liveit2win.com

If you would like to have Dr. Jerry Grillo speak at your next Conference, Business Meeting, or host a Leadership Conference at your church contact:

Fogzone Ministries
P.O. Box 3707
Hickory, NC. 28601
Email us at FZM@LIVEIT2WIN.COM
828.325.4773

[i] Dr. Mike Murdock, The Law of Recognition, 1999, The Wisdom Center, 35-36.

www.ingramcontent.com/pod-product-compliance
Lightning Source LLC
Chambersburg PA
CBHW060531100426
42743CB00009B/1494